Raga Harmony

Global violin icon Dr L. Subramaniam, is the world's leading authority of South Indian classical music and violin, having performed for more than sixty-five years now. A childhood prodigy, he was honoured with the title 'Violin Chakravarti' at the age of twenty-five. In his long and illustrious career since, Dr Subramaniam has collaborated with the greatest musicians of his time. He is the only musician who has performed/recorded Carnatic classical music, Western classical music, both orchestral and non-orchestral, and composed for, conducted and performed as a soloist with many major orchestras, scored for films and ballets, collaborated with some of the greatest musicians of his time (including George Harrison, Stevie Wonder, Yehudi Menuhin, and many others), from different genres of music including jazz, occidental, jugalbandhis with North Indian musicians and world music. He created the global fusion concept in the mid-1970s.

He has mastered various techniques and genres, explored new avenues (he was a musical advisor to Peter Brook about the sound concepts for his 'Mahabharata'), even composed music for a select few films (*Salaam Bombay* and *Mississippi Masala*, among others, and was featured as a soloist in Bernardo Bertolucci's *Little Buddha* and *Cotton Mary* of Merchant–Ivory Productions). Yet, his technical mastery finds its truest experience in the service of Carnatic music, the tradition he has inherited from his father and guru, Professor V Lakshminarayana.

He has received several awards and honours, including the coveted Padma Bhushan in 2001 and Sangeet Natak Akademi Award for 'The Most Creative Artist' in 1990 from the President of India. In recognition of his contribution to the World of Music, he has been conferred with Honorary Doctorates by Bangalore University (2003), University of Madras (2004), Sheffield University (2008), Rabindra Bharathi University (2016), ITM University (2016) and National Institute for Education and Research (2016).

L. Subramaniam

Raga Harmony

Harmonic structures
and tonalities
in Indian classical music

Published by Westland Non-Fiction, an imprint of Westland Books, a division of Nasadiya Technologies Private Limited, in 2024

No. 269/2B, First Floor, 'Irai Arul', Vimalraj Street, Nethaji Nagar, Alapakkam Main Road, Maduravoyal, Chennai 600095

Westland, the Westland logo, Westland Non-Fiction and the Westland Non-Fiction logo are the trademarks of Nasadiya Technologies Private Limited, or its affiliates.

ISBN: 9789360454715

10 9 8 7 6 5 4 3 2 1

Typeset by SÜRYA, New Delhi

Printed at Parksons Graphics Pvt. Ltd

Contents

Preface

My father and *guru* Prof. V Lakshminarayana wanted the Indian violin to reach the international stage. It was his dream to present the violin as a solo instrument in the Carnatic classical tradition and take it to audiences around the world. My father's ambition motivated me to perform not just Carnatic classical music but also present the core idea of our music—the *raga*—in different forms. I created the global fusion idiom and also composed several cross-over orchestral pieces that were played by some of the leading orchestras in prestigious venues. In some sense, it was the heart of Indian classical music being showcased globally.

In order to accomplish this, I had to develop a system that was different from the traditional Western harmony concept. My system had to be based on the melodic concept of *raga* and using the notes of the *raga*s to create combinations that would give rise to harmonies that are rich in tonality and pleasing to the ears.

As a student of Western classical composition in CalArts, I began developing a system that could integrate the melodic ideas of Indian classical music with the harmonic structure of

Western classical music. This manifested initially in my fusion compositions of the late 1970s, and then starting from Double Concerto (1983), I composed several orchestral pieces. In Fantasy on Vedic Chants (1985), for example, starting with the simple tri-tonal chant of the Vedic *mantra*s, the first movement slowly enters *Raga* Chakravakam. The second movement is based on Kiravani, and the third starts with Hamsadhvani and ends with a *ragamalika*. While this was an orchestral composition, it had a strong Indian flavour. A listener from India can relate to the mood of the *raga* while a listener from the West, who may not know anything about the *raga*, can connect with the rich harmony played by the symphony orchestra.

After close to five decades of composing and performing within the *Raga* Harmony framework, I decided to pursue a PhD so that my work could be vetted by the academic world. I wrote my doctoral thesis on this subject and the present book is an adaptation of the same. I believe it will be practically useful for all kinds of composers. Indian composers who might be hesitant to compose an orchestral composition will find it useful, as will Western composers who might be unfamiliar with the *raga* system. However, it is my fervent belief that a composer will greatly benefit by thoroughly studying both systems—studying *raga*s on the one hand and harmony and counterpoint on the other. Using the wealth of melodic content present in the *raga*s and the beauty of the harmonic structure, one will be able to create newer music and reach newer audiences.

I wish to express my gratitude to Mr. Chenraj Jain and

everyone at the Jain University for making it possible for me to pursue my doctoral studies, particularly my PhD advisor, Dr Meera Rajaram Pranesh.

My heartfelt thanks to the publishers, Westland for taking great interest in bringing out this book. I wish to thank the editors Sonia Madan and Pallavi Mohan for their thorough review of the manuscript. I also wish to thank Dr M A Madhuvanti for her initial copyediting of the manuscript.

This project could not have been completed without the help of my daughter Bindu and my disciple Hari Ravikumar. My thanks to them.

Finally, I want to thank Kavita for her patience and full support in all my activities—as well as my family, Narayana, Ambi and Mahati, for their understanding when I have not been able to spend enough time with them!

L Subramaniam

Introduction

Indian music is one of the oldest and most sophisticated types of music. In a way, it is also the most complete. It has been developed from the Vedas, which are more than 5,000 years old. Historically, Vedic hymns were chanted by male priests in temples and they formed the basis of Indian music. A scientific, intellectual and intuitive approach developed this further.

The concept of *melakarta* (parent scale) was greatly expanded on by the musician-musicologist Venkatamakhi, who came up with the system of the seventy-two parent scales. From these seventy-two parent scales, millions of scales can be derived. When it comes to rhythm, Carnatic music has a system of seven basic *tala*s that are further expanded into 175 *tala*s and *chapu tala*s.

The three most important composers, Tyagaraja, Muthuswamy Dikshitar and Shyama Shastri, collectively known as the Trinity of Carnatic music, based their compositions on the melodic and rhythmic concepts of the *melakarta* system and on the system of the seven basic *tala*s and *chapu tala*s. Other composers developed additional compositions on the same lines. Their compositions were written as vocal compositions, with a strong spiritual base. When the ensemble performed, the other melodic accompanists duplicated the melody of the soloist in unison, and no distinct instrumental music was written.

This is possibly the reason why, instead of going in the harmonic direction, Carnatic music followed a more horizontal, microtonal (*sruti*) approach to music with ornamentations (*gamakas*). Subsequently, different musical ensembles, both vocal and instrumental, took these compositions and individual performers started improvising around them. This led to *raga* improvisation and *swara kalpana* (melodic improvisation set to a *tala* cycle). Improvisation became a major vehicle of expression for musicians, and through this expression, they created their own *bani*s or identities. In addition to the distinct styles of the three composers, the same compositions were adapted to different *bani*s by individual performers. This resulted in the growth of a different melodic approach, using more ornamentation or *gamakas*, and creating different styles or identities.

On the other hand, in the West, classical music developed from monophony (plainsong), which had a spiritual basis, to polyphony. Composers also started composing for different instruments, and that led to the creation of smaller ensembles, chamber orchestras and symphony orchestras. Since they had different instruments in an ensemble setting, composers started writing distinct lines for different instruments that would complement each other and be musically pleasing. This resulted in vertical motion of the composition and the development of harmony, which became one of the central concepts of Western classical music.

In the West, the composers—some of whom were virtuosic performers—created many instrumental compositions for different instruments and went on to explore different tonalities, thereby creating an identity to their style, such as, Bach for Baroque, Mozart for Classical and Tchaikovsky for Romantic. The composers slowly began to even write the improvisational parts like the *cadenzas* in concertos (instrumental compositions for solo instruments and orchestras), where earlier the soloist was expected to improvise. So, eighteenth century onwards, improvisation in Western classical music slowly started to disappear.

By using the parent scales, it is possible to create tonalities that are identical to Western harmony. This concept, which I call '*Raga* Harmony', can be used to create major orchestral compositions. Harmonic progression, in this context, refers to the combination of notes in a successive vertical motion, in order to create polyphony underneath a melody.

With the new concept of thirty-six scales that I have presented, it is possible to create harmonic structures and harmonic tonalities with unlimited possibilities. The compositions created using *Raga* Harmony can be played by an orchestra comprising a large number of musicians, even without the individual musicians understanding the concept of *Raga* Harmony. The composer uses the concept of *Raga* Harmony and gives notated lines to each individual member of the orchestra. Thus, a composition using *Raga* Harmony can be performed by a group of 50–100 musicians, without any additional effort or knowledge on the part of those musicians, except perhaps having to practice unusual scale patterns corresponding to the *raga* scales chosen for the composition.

Background

In the past, Western composers with concrete knowledge of Western classical music have explored creating orchestral compositions using Indian influences, by either taking a scale or a rhythmic cycle. However, there have not been any orchestral compositions that combine the whole concept of Indian music, written with complete Indian tonalities, with structures that bring the tonality of the complete Western harmony.

To my knowledge, there has not been any Indian composer who studied only Indian music but could write Western orchestral compositions. Such composers have always relied on Western arrangers familiar with Western orchestral music theory and composition.

Over the last four decades, as a composer, I have developed a method of using the Indian *raga* system to create complete Western orchestral compositions and performed them with some of the world's leading orchestras. Through my own practical approach, based on the study of both Western and Indian music, I was able to devise a system which distils down the Indian *raga* system to a 36-scale concept. This system will be beneficial to both the Indian musician and the Western composer.

Highlights

1. Using only the notes of a *melakarta*, it is possible to create harmonic tonalities which can fit into the Western harmonic system.

2. Using *Raga* Harmony alone, compositions can be created with harmonic tonalities. Given that they will not follow traditional—therefore, common and, at times, predictable—harmonic progressions, it is possible that some of these harmonic tonalities would be fresh and interesting for composers. The new 36-scale concept will allow composers to create endless harmonic patterns.

3. It is possible to create complex harmonic tonalities even without knowledge of the Western system. However, an understanding of the Western system has definite advantages. For instance, it helps the composer understand which harmony in a *raga* structure may correspond to recognised Western chords. Knowing the methodology of creating harmony in the Western system will also give a definite direction in terms of harmonic progression. It will also be much easier to communicate and collaborate with another person familiar with the Western system, especially when a Western orchestra is required to perform the compositions, and when it has to be notated.

Contribution of Musicians and Scholars to the Field

In the past, Western composers, on occasion, have used Indian concepts or themes in orchestral compositions. Composers like Alan Hovanhess and Mike Powell came to India, studied Indian music and tried to adopt some basic Indian concepts in their compositions. In the 1800s, it was a fashionable practice for operas to be set in the Orient; for instance, three famous operas of the time set in the Orient are Lakme (by Leo Delibes), Le roi de Lahore/The King of Lahore (by Jules Massenet) and Les Pecheurs de Perles/The Pearl Fishers (by George Bizet). In mid-1960s, John Craig Cooper, a Fulbright scholar, came to India and added Indian influences to his compositions.

In Indian films, from the time of the music directors like Shankar–Jaikishan, a Western/orchestral colour has been added to pure Indian melodies by using Western harmonic concepts. Indeed, the music directors of the past composed Indian melodic themes often based on classical *ragas*—but during the interludes, for the background scores and under the melodies, they used Western elements. They employed Western musicians as well as music arrangers who had studied Western classical music to do this.

There have been a number of books written about Western harmony and its history by Western authors and also many Indian books written about Indian music and culture. Starting from Bharata's *Natyashastra* (fifth century BCE), some of the important Indian treatises include *Sangeeta Sudhakara* of Haripala, *Sangeeta Ratnakara* of Sarngadeva, *Swaramelakalanidhi* of Ramamatya, *Chaturdandiprakasika* of Venkatamakhi, *Sangraha Choodamani* of Govindacharya and, more recently, books by musicologist P. Sambamoorthy, who has also expounded on the concept of 5,184 *melas*.

Raga-based harmony and *raga*-based harmonic compositions have remained largely unexplored and, to my knowledge, no specific research has been done in this field. This is the first extensive study of possible harmonic tonalities that can be created using this new concept where only 36 scales—which have been developed from the *Melakarta Raga* system—cover not only Western classical possibilities but also North Indian primary scale patterns, thereby creating the scope for unlimited harmonic tonalities. What this means is that using only the *raga* system and the 36 *raga* scale patterns, full orchestral compositions can be created. This system will possibly cover all the existing harmonic tonalities used in the past, and possibly in the future.

The present work examines 5,184 *sampoorna* scales and follows the tempered system of music, which is prevalent in orchestral writing. This will make it more suitable and practically applicable, even though some musicians have experimented with a microtonal approach for smaller ensembles.

In the present work, I have taken two *melakarta ragas*, *Charukesi* and *Shanmukhapriya*, which have been used in *raga*-based harmonic compositions. I have explored the harmonic patterns that can be created using *Raga* Harmony. Taking the examples of existing compositions, I have outlined the application of *Raga* Harmony.

I have also created new compositions to show the development of a scale into a *raga*, and the creation of compositions from the 36-scale concept of *Raga* Harmony.

Overview of the Book

The first chapter 'Western Classical Music' focuses on Western classical music from its origin in single note church music through its development in major periods, namely, Baroque, Classical, Romantic and Modern Period. It also outlines scales and modes present in Western music, as well as the concept of ensembles in Indian music. The chapter concludes with the present situation of Western orchestral music, and the Indian and global influences present in contemporary orchestral compositions.

The second chapter traces the development of Indian music, from the Vedic period to the present. The focus of the chapter is on the historical development of Indian music through the Ancient, Medieval, Modern and Post-Independence periods, and on select composers who have advanced the *raga* system through their work. It lays the foundation for the next chapter, which deals with the *Mela* concept in Carnatic music.

The third chapter, '*Mela* concept in Carnatic music', analyses the evolution of *raga*s from *grama, jaati, moorchana,* by tracing their development through different treatises. It also includes the classification of *raga*s and the *Mela paddhati*. From there it moves on to the derivation of 5,184 *sampoorna* scales from 72 *melakartas*, and further expansion to 62,208 *sampoorna* scales. The chapter deals with the differences between scales and *raga*s, and how scales can be made into *raga*s. I have given examples of some scales being made into *raga*s.

The fourth chapter delves into the practical application of *Raga* Harmony, taking the examples of two *melakarta raga*s,

Charukesi and Shanmukhapriya. I have also traced a brief history of both *ragas*. In the case of the *ragas*, the harmonic structure available within each is presented, and then practically applied in a composition—Shanti Priya in the case of Charukesi and Paris Concerto in the case of Shanmukhapriya.

The fifth chapter presents an analysis of the new concept of 36 scales, its expansion first to 1,296 scales, and further expansion to 15,552 scales. It also explains how these scales can be adapted to Western music, and gives examples of compositions in the *raga* adapted from one of those scales. The chapter also touches upon the *Madhyama grama* concept in Indian music, where the scale can contain two *madhyamas*. The new 36 scale concept can use two *madhayamas* and a *panchama*.

The conclusion discusses the main points of the work, and presents the new concept of 36 scales, which can potentially fit all existing scales into its framework. It also opens up doors for the creation of new and fresh harmonies. Using this system of 36 scales, it is possible for someone from the West to understand the placement of notes within a *raga,* and potentially be able to comprehend and play all *ragas*. It can also help any musician develop the technical skill to master any combination of notes in any *raga.*

My Orchestral Compositions

I have written close to 20 compositions for full orchestras, and numerous other works for ensembles. The complete list is given in the Appendix.

My compositions created using the *Raga* Harmony concept

have been performed close to 200 times by leading orchestras around the world, including the New York Philharmonic, the London Philharmonic, the Kirov (Mariinsky) Orchestra, Swiss Romande, the London Symphony Orchestra, the Brandenburg Symphony Orchestra, Orchestra Nationale de Lille, the Beijing Symphony Orchestra, the Oslo Philharmonic Orchestra, the Lancaster Symphony, The Transvaal Philharmonic, The Kwa-Zulu Natal Philharmonic, the Yomiuri Nippon Orchestra, the Tivoli Gardens Symphony, the New Zealand Symphony, the Budapest Symphony, the Singapore Symphony, the Leipzig Philharmonic and the Royal Oman Symphony Orchestra.

I have worked with some of the world's greatest conductors such as, Maestro Zubin Mehta, Maestro Vladimir Fedoseyev, Maestro Jean-Claude Casadesus, Maestro Michael Helmrath, Maestro Christian Eggen, Maestro Svend Skibber, Maestro Stephen Gunzenhauser, Maestro Phillipe Bender, Maestro Simon Wright, Maestro Tan Lihua, Maestro Li Xincao and Maestro Michael Koehler.

I have received a number of commissions and awards from orchestras around the world including the Norwegian NRK P2 Award/Commission. My *Global Symphony* was broadcast simultaneously across 28 nations to millions of people.

My works have recently been published by Schott Music.

In addition to this, I have used the concept of *Raga* Harmony in several of my fusion compositions, collaborating with musicians from various genres.

This book aims to open possibilities for both Western classical composers and Indian musicians, to write orchestral compositions with new harmonies. My research is based on practical work done by me over decades and has broader applications for all composers who can potentially learn this new system and apply it to their own orchestral composing.

My research also opens up tremendous possibilities for *raga* creation through the scales that have been identified. Using this approach, millions of *raga*s, both *sampoorna* and *janya*, can be created.

1

Western Classical Music

In general, Western culture has grown from the Mesopotamian (3500 BCE), Greek, Roman and Egyptian civilisations. Western music, too, is believed to have ancient roots, with some echoes of ancient music being seen in the Western tradition.

The origins of Western classical music are most often tied to Christianity and the Church. It is, however, worthwhile to note that certain Christian practices, including the singing of psalms, were inherited from the Judaic traditions that preceded them. In Jewish synagogues, a choir of Levites (members of the priestly class) would sing psalms accompanied by harps, psalteries (plucked zither), trumpets and cymbals. Later on, responsorial singing (alternate singing between the choir and a soloist), common in the Jewish liturgy, was also introduced into Christian worship.

Music of the Early Church

In the fourth century, there were changes both in the church and the music of the church. The language of the church in the West was changed from Greek to Latin. Moreover, different centres of Christianity in Europe developed separate musical traditions, as they had a large degree of independence. In this manner, many varieties of plainchant were developed in different centres. Plainchant or plainsong were the unaccompanied monophonic melodies to which texts of the Roman Catholic liturgy were sung. The melodic range was limited. Plainchant was passed down through an oral tradition.

In Milan developed the Milanese or Ambrosian chant, in Visgothic Spain the Mozarabic chant, and in France the Gallican chant. The unification of different styles of church music was brought about by Pope Gregory, who, in addition to setting up a *schola cantorum*, or music school, in Rome, also created the Gregorian chant.

Music and Philosophy

As music became a great support to the institution of the church and gained an important position in church services, many philosophers continued to postulate the effects of music.

St Augustine (354–430 CE) wrote that music had the power to influence action in the direction of good or evil.

Boethius (c. 480–524 CE), in *De Institutione Musica*, postulated that music is firstly a force pervading the whole universe, an element that controls the union of body and soul.

Notation in Early Music

Until the seventh century, when *neumes* were introduced, plainchants in the churches of Western Europe were passed down through an oral tradition. Neumes were indicators of melody written above the text or the music, and indicated the pitch (it represented up to four notes) and the duration of the note.

In the eleventh century, coloured lines were devised to indicate pitch. The Italian monk Guido D'Arezzo created a four-line staff system for accurate notation and introduced solmisation, which used names such as ut, re, me, ta and so for notes. His system was based on six-note scales or hexachords.

Precise representation of the duration of the notes came after the thirteenth century in polyphonic systems of the Notre Dame composers in Paris.

From Monophony to Polyphony and Harmony

Polyphony refers to there being more than one melodic line in a composition. This means all singers are not in unison. Polyphony developed gradually, and monophony and polyphony co-existed for a very long time.

St Ambrose and St Gregory started using polyphony by adding octaves, and then intervals of a fourth or a fifth, where the two melodies would move in similar motion.

During the time of Guido D'Arezzo, the second voice (which was the perfect fifth below the main melody) started holding the note when the melody moved below F (because it was not comfortable for the voice to reach the lower note). This resulted in an oblique motion between the voices. He also had a voice singing in intervals of a third.

Following this, other composers tried to end the song in unison. The upper voice moved down to the tonic to end the composition and the lower voice moved up to reach the tonic, which resulted in harmonic contrary motion.

In the early ninth century, *Musica Enchiradis*, a manual for singers, had the original plainchant melody accompanied by another vocal melody. This led to singing in octaves—one octave below the main voice and one octave above the second voice. This early polyphony was known as organum. It continued to develop in France and Spain, where the lower tenor voice held the plainchant and the upper voice or *duplum* was given an ornamented melody and had greater freedom of expression. In the early twelfth century, the Notre Dame Cathedral became the focal point for the development of musical activity in Western Europe.

Secular music emerged around the ninth or tenth century with minstrels (travelling musicians). The twelfth century also saw the arrival of troubadours (poet musicians).

It is worthwhile to note that the use of instruments was discouraged in the early music of the Church, because instruments were associated with 'pagan' beliefs. Instruments were reintroduced into the music of the church only after the development of complex polyphony, and many of the instruments used were brought to Europe by the Crusaders.

Thirteenth to Fifteenth Century CE

Ars Nova or New Art was the name given to the new music that developed in France in the fourteenth century. It was meant to replace *Ars Antiqua* or Old Art of the thirteenth century. *Ars Nova* used more varied rhythmic patterns that included a greater use of duple time and the introduction of the minim.

Guillaume de Machaut was a leading composer of the *Ars Nova* style. He is credited with writing the first polyphonic mass. Although, at that time, most non-spiritual music was condemned by the Church, most of his music was composed to be heard outside the church.

Around the same time, secular music also began to develop in Italy. Francesco Landini (1335–1397 CE), the leading composer of his day, exclusively wrote secular music. His innovative use of both harmony and cadence was a departure from the previous norm. In the middle of the fourteenth century, Italian music also began to be influenced by *Ars Nova*.

Not much is known of English music in the early Middle Ages. John Dunstable (1385–1453 CE) was the first English composer to gain European recognition.

Although very little music from the early Middle Ages has survived, the depiction of instruments in artworks and literature shows that instruments played a role in the social activities of that time. Towards the later part of the Middle Ages, the use of instruments in the Church became more widespread.

Also, during the fourteenth and fifteenth centuries, the French system of notation was developed.

The Renaissance

The fifteenth and sixteenth centuries saw great change in Europe, from the Renaissance to the Protestant Reformation and then, the Counter-Reformation.

In the fifteenth century, a new kind of musician—the professional composer—began moving from place to place. They were highly paid and honoured at the Italian courts and the papal chapels. Composers from Italy and travelling musicians from all over Europe brought their music to England in the middle of the sixteenth century, especially the Italian forms (madrigals, ballets and conzonets). The year 1600 CE marked the most drastic break in the development of European polyphony, which became a decisive element and the basis for Protestant Church music from Schutz to Bach.

The spread of music was also helped by the invention of the Gutenberg press. During the Reformation, the music in Germany developed greatly. Martin Luther himself possessed great musical skill and wanted the entire Church congregation to sing during the Protestant services.

In pre-Baroque times, composers were regularly commissioned to write compositions for instrumental ensembles to be played at church events. This led to the development of instrumental music. During that period, the most frequently used instruments were those belonging to the string family (violin, viola and cello).

Baroque Period

The term 'baroque' refers to music, art and architecture that was produced in the period starting from the end of the sixteenth century going up to the middle of the eighteenth century. Some major composers of the Baroque era were Johann Sebastian Bach, George Frideric Handel, Antonio Vivaldi, Henry Purcell, Claudio Monteverdi and Johann Pachelbel.

The Baroque period is often divided into early, middle and late periods.

During the Baroque period, there was widespread use of figured bass. With figured bass, numbers or symbols were placed above the bassline in music. Keyboard instrument players read the figured bass and decided what intervals they should play above each bass note and improvise chord voicing.

Moreover, during this period, composers began working on harmonic progressions and on the development of tonality within a composition, which means the setting of a composition in a particular key.

Claudio Monteverdi is credited with developing basso continuo. During the Baroque era, musicians were expected to be able to improvise solo melodic lines and the accompaniment parts. Concerts were accompanied by a basso continuo group of chord-playing instrumentalists improvising the chords from a figured bass part while a group of bass instruments (viola, cello and double bass) played the bassline.

In the Baroque era, ornamentation, which was usually improvised by performers, became more complex. There were also developments in music notation and instrument-playing techniques. Baroque music expanded the size, range and complexity of instrumental performance. Further, it established the mixed vocal/instrumental forms of opera, cantata and oratorio, and the instrumental forms of the solo concerto and sonata as musical genres. Many musical terms and concepts from this era, such as toccata, fugue and concerto grosso, are still in use.

The greatest musical invention during the Baroque period was the opera. When the first commercially run opera house opened in Venice in 1637 CE, opera established itself as a popular baroque form of entertainment. One of the most important opera composers of the time was Monteverdi, whose *Orfeo* was released in 1607 CE.

Middle Baroque Music (1630–1680 CE)

During the Age of Absolutism, Louis XIV of France became a model for the rest of Europe. The realities of rising Church and State patronage created a demand for organised public music, as the increasing availability of instruments created a demand for chamber music.

The middle Baroque period in Italy was defined by the emergence of a new concept of melody and harmony that elevated the status of the music to one of equality with words. Prior to this, words had been considered pre-eminent. In line with this shift, the 1630s saw the rise of the vocal styles of cantata, oratorio and opera.

Late Baroque Music (1680–1730 CE)

The work of George Frideric Handel, Johann Sebastian Bach and their contemporaries, including Domenico Scarlatti, Antonio Vivaldi, Georg Philipp Telemann and others, advanced the Baroque era to its climax.

A continuous worker, Handel borrowed from other composers and often 'recycled' his own material. He was also known for reworking pieces such as the famous oratorio, *Messiah*, which premiered in 1742 CE, for available singers and musicians.

Vivaldi wrote (secular) instrumental compositions like concertos, sonatas and concerto for two violins. This provided a strong foundation for many other instrumental compositions. Bach and Handel not only gave Baroque harmony a definite shape and form, but with their creative genius, they gave a definitive identity to the Baroque period. Bach created monumental choral works like *St. Matthew Passion* and *Mass in B minor*, and wrote concerto *grossos*, which involved multiple soloists as opposed to concertos, which had only one soloist. Both Bach and Handel also wrote sonatas, symphonies and concertos.

From this point onward, instrumental music started flourishing and developing at a faster pace because it was patronised not only by the churches but also by private patrons like royalty, noblemen and wealthy individuals.

The composition of the Baroque orchestra included woodwinds (two flutes, two oboes, two bassoons), brass (two horns [in any key], two trumpets [in any key]), percussion (timpani), keyboards (harpsichord), strings (six violins I, six violins II, four violas, two violoncellos and bass).

Classical Period

Classical music has a lighter, clearer texture than Baroque music and is less complex. Focusing on a light style and elegance, it uses a clear melody line over a subordinate chordal accompaniment.

During the Classical period, variety and contrast within a piece became more pronounced than ever before and the orchestra increased in size, range and power. The piano replaced the harpsichord as the main keyboard solo instrument. This new instrument also influenced compositions, because the piano was more capable of playing dynamics and sustains. Importance was given to instrumental music—the main kinds were the sonata, the trio, the string quartet, the symphony and the solo concerto, which featured a virtuoso solo performer playing the violin, piano, flute or any another instrument, accompanied by an orchestra.

The best-known composers from this period are Joseph Haydn, Wolfgang Amadeus Mozart, Ludwig van Beethoven and Franz Schubert.

Ludwig van Beethoven is also regarded as a Romantic composer or a composer who was a part of the transition to the Romantic period. The period is sometimes referred to as the era of Viennese Classic or Classicism (German: *Wiener Klassik*), since Wolfgang Amadeus Mozart, Joseph Haydn, Antonio Salieri and Ludwig van Beethoven all worked at one time or the other in Vienna, and Franz Schubert was born there.

Classical music was still tightly linked to the aristocratic court culture and was supported by absolute monarchies. In contrast with the richly layered music of the Baroque era, Classical music moved towards simplicity rather than complexity. Chords became a much more prevalent feature of music, even if they interrupted the melodic smoothness of a single part. As a result, the tonal structure of a piece of music became more audible.

As the eighteenth century progressed, the nobility became the primary patrons of instrumental music, while public taste increasingly preferred light, funny comic operas. This led to changes in the way music was performed. In Classical compositions, all parts were specifically noted, though not always notated. By 1800 CE, basso continuo was practically extinct, except for the occasional use of a pipe organ continuo part in a religious mass in the early 1800s.

Economic changes also had the effect of altering the balance of availability and quality of musicians. While in the late Baroque era, a major composer had the entire musical resources of a town to draw on, the musical forces available at an aristocratic hunting lodge or a small court were smaller and more fixed to their level of ability. This was a spur towards having simpler parts for ensemble musicians to play and, in the case of a resident virtuoso group, a spur to writing spectacular, idiomatic parts for certain instruments—as in the case of the Mannheim orchestra—or virtuoso solo parts for particularly skilled violinists or flautists.

In addition, the appetite of audiences for a continual supply of new music carried over from the Baroque period. This meant that works had to be performable with, at best, one or two rehearsals. Indeed, even after 1790 CE, Mozart has written about 'the' rehearsal, with the implication that his concerts would have only one rehearsal.

In the Classical era, there was greater emphasis on notating the line for dynamics and phrasing. It became common for composers to indicate where they wanted performers to play ornaments such as trills or turns. The simplification of musical texture made such instrumental detail more important, and also made the use of characteristic rhythms more important.

Forms such as the concerto and sonata were more heavily defined and given more specific rules. Moreover, the symphony, popularly attributed to Joseph Haydn, was created in this period. The concerto *grosso* (a concerto for more than one musician), a very popular form in the Baroque era, began to be replaced by the solo concerto (a concerto featuring only one soloist, accompanied by orchestra). Given that Classical concertos only had a single soloist, composers began to place more importance on the particular soloist's ability to show off virtuoso skills, with challenging, fast scale, arpeggio runs. There were, of course, some concerti *grossi* that remained, the most famous of which was Mozart's *Sinfonia Concertante for Violin and Viola in E flat Major*.

The orchestra increased in size and range; the harpsichord or pipe organ's basso continuo role in the orchestra gradually fell out of use between 1750 and 1800 CE. Also, woodwinds became a self-contained section, consisting of clarinets, oboes, flutes and bassoons.

Over the Classical period, the pieces became richer, more sonorous and more powerful.

Haydn's great contribution to music was a way of composing, a way of structuring works, which was at the same time in accord with the governing aesthetic of the new style. A younger contemporary, Wolfgang Amadeus Mozart brought his genius to Haydn's ideas and applied them to the opera and the virtuoso concerto. Haydn spent much of his working life as a court composer but Mozart wanted public success in the concert life of cities, playing for the general public. This meant he needed to write operas, and write and perform virtuoso pieces. Mozart also had a taste for more chromatic chords, a greater love for creating a welter of melodies in a single work, and a more Italianate sensibility in music as a whole. He found, in Haydn's music and later in his study of the polyphony of J.S. Bach, the means to discipline and to enrich his artistic gifts.

Mozart rapidly came to the attention of Haydn, who hailed the new composer, studied his works, and considered the younger man his only true peer in music. In Mozart, Haydn found a greater range of instrumentation, dramatic effect and melodic resources. The learning relationship moved in both directions. Mozart also had great respect for the older, more experienced composer, and sought to learn from him.

Mozart's arrival in Vienna in 1780 CE brought acceleration in the development of the Classical style. It was during this decade that public taste began, increasingly, to recognise that Haydn and Mozart had reached a high standard of composition. By the time Mozart turned twenty-five, in 1781 CE, the dominant styles of Vienna were recognisably connected to the emergence in the 1750s of the early Classical style. By the end of the 1780s, changes in performance practice, the relative standing of instrumental and vocal music, technical demands on musicians, and stylistic unity had become established in the composers who imitated Mozart and Haydn. During this decade, Mozart composed his most famous operas, his six late symphonies that helped to redefine the genre, and a string of piano concerti that still stand at the pinnacle of these forms.

In the 1790s, a new generation of composers, born around 1770 CE, emerged. The most fateful of the new generation was Ludwig van Beethoven, who launched his numbered works in 1794 CE with a set of three piano trios, which remain in the repertoire.

The direct influence of Baroque music continued to fade: the figured bass grew less prominent as a means of holding a performance together while the performance practices of the mid-eighteenth century continued to die out. However, at the same time, complete editions of Baroque masters began to become available, and the influence of Baroque style continued to grow, particularly in the ever more expansive use of brass.

Another feature of the period was the growing number of performances where the composer was not present. This led to increased detail and specificity in notation; for example, there were fewer 'optional' parts that stood apart from the main score.

The force of these shifts became apparent with Beethoven's Symphony No. 3, given the name *Eroica*, which is Italian for 'heroic'. As with Stravinsky's *The Rite of Spring*, *Eroica* may not have been the first in all of its innovations, but its aggressive use of every part of the Classical style set it apart from its contemporary works: in length, ambition and harmonic resources.

However, the forces destined to end the hold of the Classical style gathered strength in the works of many composers, particularly Beethoven. The most commonly cited force at play was that of harmonic innovation. Also important was the increasing focus on having a continuous and rhythmically uniform accompanying figuration: Beethoven's *Moonlight Sonata* was the model for hundreds of later pieces—where the shifting movement of a rhythmic figure provides much of the drama and interest to the work, while a melody drifts above it. Greater knowledge of works, greater instrumental expertise, an increasing variety of instruments, the growth of concert societies, and the unstoppable dominance of the increasingly more powerful piano (which was given a bolder, louder tone by technological developments such as the use of steel strings, heavy cast-iron frames and sympathetically vibrating strings) all created a huge audience for sophisticated music. All of these trends contributed to the shift to the 'Romantic' style.

Differentiating between these two styles is very difficult: some sections of Mozart's later works, taken alone, are indistinguishable in harmony and orchestration from music written eighty years later—in fact, some composers continued to write in normative Classical styles even into the early twentieth century.

Vienna's fall as the most important musical centre for orchestral composition marked the Classical style's final eclipse as well as the end of its continuous organic development by way of one composer learning in close proximity to others. Franz Liszt and Frédéric Chopin visited Vienna when they were young, but then moved on to other cities.

In the early twentieth century, renewed interest in the formal balance and restraint of the eighteenth-century Classical music led to the development of the so-called Neo-classical style. The Neo-classical style counted among its proponents Stravinsky and Prokofiev, at least at certain points in their careers.

The instrumentation of the early Classical orchestra included two flutes, two oboes, two clarinets, two bassoons, two horns, two trumpets, timpani and strings. The Late Classical (or Beethoven) orchestra saw the addition of a clarinet, cor anglais, piccolo, three trombones, tuba, four horns and percussion instruments like cymbals, triangle and bass drum.

Romantic Period

The contributions of Beethoven made a nice bridge from the Classical to the Romantic era. He took the music to different heights with his emotional content, harmony and orchestration.

His violin concerto in D became an important composition for all classical violinists not only due to its melodic richness but also due to its emotional content. Although rooted in the Classical period (it is also believed that Beethoven approached Mozart for training and was turned down, finally learning from Haydn), he took the level of composition to the next higher level—the Romantic period. It was believed that Beethoven had a copy of the *Upanishads* and the *Vedas*.

Subsequently, there were many other Romantic composers who contributed immensely to the development of Western music, like Schubert, Brahms, Liszt and Tchaikovsky. The composer Richard Wagner's music almost led to the culmination of the Romantic period. His compositions were so overpowering in the Romantic style that composers started looking towards different directions to create individualistic styles.

Many early-nineteenth–century composers were also influenced by the literary Romantics such as Johann Wolfgang von Goethe. Romantic composers used Goethe's poems as a source of lyrics for songs that were sung by a solo singer accompanied by a pianist. These songs accompanied by piano were called Lieder. Robert Schumann (1810–1856 CE) wrote many important Lieder. Romantic composers wrote many programmatic orchestra pieces, where the composer tried to tell a story or 'illustrate' a scene using music. An example of this is *Symphonie fantastique* composed in 1830 CE by Hector Berlioz (1803–1869 CE), which uses purely instrumental music to depict a story about a young artist who is tormented by his love for a woman, so much so that he takes opium, has hallucinations, and is eventually sent to the gallows for execution.

The Romantic era was also an important time for short, yet emotionally dramatic piano pieces. The pianist-composer Frédéric Chopin (1810–1849 CE) wrote piano pieces in the form of etudes, ballades and mazurkas. Even though Chopin did not give poetic titles to his piano pieces, like Berlioz did for his *Symphonie fantastique*, Chopin's piano pieces contain intense emotion and drama, from a musical sense.

Opera, which was very important during the Classical music era, continued to maintain its importance during the Romantic era. Giuseppe Verdi (1813–1901 CE) wrote operas from the 1840s to the 1880s. Verdi popularised the bel canto style of writing for opera singers. 'Bel canto' is an Italian term for 'beautifully sung'. Verdi's operas used large choruses of singers to accompany the solo singers. While eighteenth-century recitatives in opera were just accompanied by basso continuo (typically harpsichord and cello), Verdi used the full orchestra to accompany his nineteenth-century recitative passages.

Along with Verdi, the other composer who dominated opera during the Romantic era was the German composer Richard Wagner (1813–1883 CE). Wagner operas were often based on Teutonic legends. Wagner aimed to have vocal melodies, orchestral parts and other dramatic elements all fused into one whole, which he called Gesamtkunstwerk, a German term that means 'total art work'. Wagner believed that the orchestra should play a very important role in opera. He gave the orchestra leitmotifs to play, and each leitmotif was associated with a specific theme, such as love or death.

The Romantic orchestra has a fixed brass section of 4-2-3-1. Woodwinds like the piccolo, cor anglais and bass clarinet were used more regularly. From a strength of thirty to forty members in the Classical era, the orchestra grew to seventy members in the Romantic era, and the need for a conductor arose.

Impressionism and Serialism

Impressionism in music was a movement among various composers of Western classical music—mainly during the late nineteenth and early twentieth centuries—whose music focused on suggestion and atmosphere, conveying the moods and emotions aroused by the subject rather than a detailed tone-picture.

Claude Debussy and Maurice Ravel are two of the leading figures of Impressionism in music, though Debussy rejected this label. He started using sequences of intervals like 2nds and 4ths and clusters of notes to create his style. He was also influenced by Eastern music (like the Indonesian Gamelan), which he had heard in Paris, and created whole tone series influenced by Impressionistic painters. He used block chords of harmony with a modal flavour based on the whole tone scale. He was an innovator. The whole tone scale is one of the derived *janya ragas* (which has six notes) of Carnatic classical music. He also used five-note scales. The full tone scale that was used by Debussy fits into one of the derived scales (*janya ragas*) in Carnatic classical music. The name of the *raga* is Gopriya, derived from the 62nd *mela* (Rishabhapriya). In the full tone scale, whichever note is the tonic note (Sa), the scale will be the same by shifting the tonic from Sa to Ri. In other words, it will still be a full tone scale. Whichever note is the tonic, the corresponding *raga* will be the same.

Debussy's Impressionist works typically evoked a mood, feeling, atmosphere, or scene by creating musical images through characteristic motifs, harmony, exotic scales (for example, whole tone scale, pentatonic scales), instrumental timbre and other elements, whereas Ravel's Impressionist or symbolist works are essentially represented in a more precise and intelligible way.

Following Debussy and Ravel, Arnold Schoenberg started working differently, in the atonal style, where all the semitones were arranged in a sequence, and were used without giving any importance to any key signatures or tonal centres. In this method, known as Serialism, the twelve notes of an octave were all given equal importance, so as to break the major/minor chordal concept, and in a composition, in whichever order the composer used the twelve tones, the same sequence was repeated horizontally or vertically by breaking away from the concept of tonalism.

Alexander Scriabin (1872–1915 CE) was another composer of the time. In 1908 CE, for Prometheus, he created a 'mystic chord' by using a note and an augmented fourth, a perfect fourth, an augmented fourth, a perfect fourth, a perfect fourth (by using sixths) C F# Bb E A D. He used fourths and even seconds to build chords achieving what has been called Impressionist tonalities. In 1908 CE, he came under the influence of theosophy and mysticism, and developed the mystic chord, a series of fourths. The scale of Prometheus is the 64th *melakarta raga* Vachaspati.

Holst wrote *Opera di Camera*, and in Act 1 Op. 25, the libretto was taken from Mahabharata in Sanskrit. The three characters were Savitri (the soprano), Satyavan (the tenor) and Death (the baritone).

Modern Period

Musicologist Carl Dahlhaus describes Modernism as '(a)n obvious point of historical discontinuity ... The "breakthrough" of Mahler, Strauss, and Debussy implies a profound historical transformation ... If we were to search for a name to convey the breakaway mood of the 1890s (a mood symbolised musically by the opening bars of Strauss's *Don Juan*) but without imposing a fictitious unity of style on the age, we could do worse than revert to Hermann Bahr's term "modernism" and speak of a stylistically open-ended "modernist music" extending (with some latitude) from 1890 CE to the beginnings of our own 20th century modern music in 1910 CE.'

Modern/*Avant Garde* music led to composers like John Cage. In 1952 CE, John Cage made a reference to the white canvases of the New York painter Robert Rauschenberg in his notorious 4'33" in which a pianist sits at the piano for 4 minutes and 33 seconds without playing a note.

Composers also took to using pre-recorded tape music along with live music. Compositions started being written giving more freedom to the artists, since only certain signals or signs were indicated in the compositions, over which artists were expected to freely express themselves. On the other hand, people like Lou Harrison, who was influenced by Gamelan, created compositions with different tonal systems, where an octave was divided into four or five equal spaces, which may have sounded out of tune to an uninitiated audience that was used to the tempered system.

There were also instances during the *Avant Garde* time where the form of composition included breaking a Steinway piano with a hammer and sawing it apart (which resulted in an injury to performer Karl-Erik Welin).

I have had the opportunity to listen to a modern piece in recent years at Royaumont where a wooden chair was moved back and forth to create a scratchy sound, another that imitated the sound of vomiting and a third that involved hitting the body of the instrument and creating sounds with the beads the performer was wearing around his neck. I was also witness to a performance by the noted violinist Arve Tellefsen playing a piece by a Norwegian composer. He made sounds by tapping his feet on the floor and creating other verbal sounds (*tok tok*) while playing. All this shows composers trying to break the concept of tonality and melodies, and stretching their imagination to create tonalities which could be considered non-musical by many but had a limited following of their own. None of the composers, to my knowledge, could establish themselves as big as Bach, Beethoven and Mozart. Studies have shown that *Avant Garde*, Modern music, New Music and the like are of interest to barely 0.4 per cent of the population.

Béla Bartók created compositions based on Hungarian folk music which had odd rhythms and different intervals in a scale that created very interesting harmony. Gypsy violinist and composer János Bihari also influenced a number of composers, including Beethoven. It is believed that gypsies migrated from

India and had Indian cultural roots. Their music also reflected to some extent the flavour and colour of Indian music. Some of the scales which were used are strongly Indian.

There were also composers who were fascinated by Indian music, Messiaen being one. He was influenced by the sounds of nature and birds. Composer Alan Hovhaness visited India on a Fulbright scholarship, studied the veena, participated in the Madras Music Festival in 1959-60 CE and composed *Madras Sonata*, *Vishnu Symphony* and *Arjuna*.

The next turning point was the minimalistic approach. One of the important composers of the movement, Terry Riley studied Indian music under Pandit Pran Nath. His composition *In C* is a landmark piece in the Minimalistic style. Other composers like Philip Glass have also had very strong Indian influences. These are some of the names which have become important in the Western music arena, but there were other musicians who also tried to incorporate Indian influences in other forms of music like jazz.

It is evident that Western music composers have looked for external influences at different points throughout history. The twentieth century witnessed the introduction of saxophone, piano and ethnic percussion instruments into orchestral music.

Scales and Modes in Western Music

In Western music, there are seven modes, which can be derived by using only the white notes on the piano:

Table 1: Scales and Modes in Western Music

Tonic	Notes	Name	Corresponding *Raga*
C	CDEFGAB	Ionian	Shankarabharanam
D	DEFGABC	Dorian	Kharaharapriya
E	EFGABCD	Phrygian	Todi
F	FGABCDE	Lydian	Kalyani
G	GABCDEF	Mixolydian	Harikambhoji
A	ABCDEFG	Aeolian	Natabhairavi
B	BCDEFGA	Locrian	Derived scale using both perfect fourth (*shuddha madhyamam*) and augmented fourth (*prati madhyamam*) without a fifth

Western music uses the concept of major scales and minor scales. The minor scales could be harmonic or melodic minor. Harmonic minor corresponds to Kiravani, as it uses a minor sixth and a major seventh and in the case of melodic minor, the ascending or the *arohana* uses a major sixth (*chatussruti dhaivata*) and a major seventh (*kakali nishadha*) while the descending *avarohana* uses a minor seventh (*kaishiki nishadha*) and a minor sixth (*shuddha dhaivata*). The third scale is a natural minor, which has a minor sixth (*shuddha dhaivata*) and minor seventh (*kaishiki nidshadha*) both while ascending and descending. Applying this to each of the twelve semitones (in an octave) forty-eight scales (twelve major and thirty-six minor) can be obtained.

If we use the enharmonic (same notes with different names) equivalents (for example, Bb = A#), we can get more.

In Western music so far, in commonly described scales and theory, one major scale with no sharps and flats is C major, then using one to seven sharps, we can get seven major scales. Using one to seven flats, we can get seven major scales. For these fifteen scales, there are relative minor scales, which start three semitones lower, from the sixth degree. There are, in the same way, fifteen minor scales. Relative minor scales are normally the natural minor.

Out of these two sets, three overlap practically. Theoretically, you can get more enharmonically equivalent scales; for example, C## = D, D## = E, E# = F, F## = G, G## = A, A ## = B, B# = C.

The Concept of Orchestra in Indian Music

Even today, during the Tyagaraja festival in Thiruvaiyaru, there are hundreds of people singing Tyagaraja *kriti*s with hundreds of instrumentalists and percussionists following in unison, but the number of artists involved cannot make it a symphonic choral work. There have been mentions of ensembles like *kuthapa* (instrumental ensembles) in ancient treatises of India. There were strong instrumental ensembles, which played during temple processions or in certain celebrations held in the royal palaces, but there were small ensembles playing certain instrumental pieces as a part of the entertainment.

If you talk about a Western orchestra, even in earlier Baroque and pre-Baroque times, there were strings, woodwinds and figured bass played by keyboards. Specific parts were written for different instruments and the range covered by this ensemble was much wider than an ensemble supporting vocalists where the range was usually less than two octaves. In the West, at the end of the Classical period and the beginning of Romantic period, composers like Beethoven and Wagner used major orchestral compositions and supplemented them with huge vocal choirs, where the choir was a part of the orchestra and supported it. Bach also wrote major choral works like *St. Matthew Passion* and *Mass in B minor*. The other form that was also developed in the West was the opera form where music and theatre complemented and supplemented each other. There was a storyline, and lyrics were written as libretto where the actors sang and acted, telling the story in a musical form by singing and acting. The orchestral support was normally in the background and also came in during an overture before the opera started. In many cases, the orchestra was not on the main stage but in a pit. We cannot say we had operas in Indian music. In the North, there was *Natya Sangeet*, where *Ramayana* and *Mahabharata* were acted and sung with a small ensemble backing them up. It is in no way comparable to symphonic orchestral composition in Western music.

Indian and Global Influences on Western Classical Music

In the case of Western music, after every one or one and a half century, there were visible and audible changes, such as the movement from prehistoric monophony to polyphony (from Baroque: Vivaldi, Bach, Handel, Haydn), then the onset of the Classical period of Mozart, to the Romantic period of Beethoven and Mendelssohn. Subsequently, Impressionistic, *Avante Garde*, twelve-tone and many other composers have been influenced by Indian music, even creating operas like *Lakmé* and compositions like *Madras Symphony*. It is also believed that during Beethoven's time, he had the *Upanishads* and the *Vedas* in his collection. In the twentieth century, the Minimalistic concept was started by Terry Riley (especially composition in C), who had trained in Indian classical music under Pandit Pran Nath. Phillip Glass was also influenced by Indian culture and this reflects in the compositions he wrote, like *Satyagraha*.

These days, because of modern internet technology, people are able to hear different cultures and different styles of music simultaneously, and there is a trend to incorporate different elements to create flavours of other cultures (a global flavour) in many compositions by many composers. This also opens up different styles of music to global listeners and has a global appeal. But it has to be done with proper knowledge so that there is a theoretical and scientific method behind this kind of composition for future generations to refer to and understand. So far, individual composers have tried to do it in their own way.

Similarly, in non-Western cultures, particularly in India, people have attempted to do orchestral compositions with the help of a third party who is familiar with orchestration and harmony by providing them with their Indian thoughts and melodies, asking the third party to create compositions for them in which they can feature as soloists, and which they can call their own compositions. This is also partly because of the influence of Bollywood where many composers have written melodies for songs which are picturised but have depended on arrangers who are primarily familiar with Western music (but are often without much knowledge of the *raga* or *melakarta* concepts). The use of orchestral arrangers in Bollywood has been prevalent for a long time, and this was much more prominent during the time of music directors like Shankar–Jaikishan, R. D. Burman and Laxmikant–Pyarelal. Some of the classical soloists have used the same method of giving some Indian melodies and depending on Western (trained) orchestral composers or arrangers to orchestrate for them and calling it their own compositions.

In the West, composers—from as early as Purcell to most of the great twentieth-century composers—have not only written the themes but also orchestrated their compositions. Every note was written by them and became a true composition of the composer. This is missing in India. This is because neither do the composers have enough opportunities to gain this kind of knowledge nor do they have the desire to do something different from others which can arouse curiosity among listeners. If this were not the case, it might have reached more people (and possibly led to the sale of more recordings or an increase in popularity). Also, institutions like recording companies or publishing companies in India usually suggest that composers do these things only for marketing and financial benefits.

If a method and concept become available which will open up the doors not only for non-Westerners to create Western compositions, but also for Western musicians to use other tonalities, then it would be possible to create truly global compositions.

This would be the perfect time to experiment with an unlimited possibility of Indian scales using clusters of notes from the unlimited Indian scales, and also triads, seventh and eleventh chords which are part of the Western harmony. In addition to that, composers will also be able to create sounds, which have not yet been used so far, in the Western harmonic structure. The *raga* system of Indian music is so vast that a single individual cannot master it in one lifetime. So, for composers, there will be a continuous outflow of material available for hundreds of years to come.

2

Indian Classical Music

Indian music has developed over thousands of years. It has a number of complexities, which makes it impossible to condense it into a single chapter. The overview presented here is with the intent to provide a baseline over which my research was conducted. The focus of this chapter is on the history and the current state of Indian classical music, while the next chapter focuses on the crucial factors that have helped shape the *raga* system and Carnatic music into its present-day form.

Indian classical music is one of the most complex systems of music in the world, with a highly developed melodic and rhythmic structure. It does not owe its origins to folk music, although it may have, at some point, been influenced by it.

Traditionally, music was given the first and most important position among the sixty-four arts in ancient India. Music is deeply involved with religion, ceremonies and important life events.

History and Development

In Hindu philosophy, music is considered to be a way to attain salvation, and there is a strong connection between music and the divine. Many of the Carnatic composers were actually saint-poets, whose compositions were spontaneous offerings to the Supreme, created in a temple or in a prayer setting (as opposed to a performance setting). Classical Indian music was traditionally passed down in the oral tradition.

The history of Indian music is broadly divided into four periods:

1. The Ancient period (from prehistoric times to 400 CE)
2. The Medieval period (fifth century CE to fifteenth century CE)
3. The Modern period (sixteenth century CE to mid-twentieth century)
4. The post-Independence period (mid-twentieth century onwards)

In general, the development of Indian music can be traced through important milestones: literature, treatises on music, inscriptions, and the musicologists and composers who have shaped, systematised and moulded the music into what it is today.

The Ancient Period

Vedas

Indian music has its origins in the *Vedas*. The four *Vedas* are also known as *sruti* or revealed divine truth, and contain thousands of Sanskrit hymns. They were passed down through the oral tradition, and committed to writing much later. Vedic texts and traditions remain unchanged to this day.

The four *Vedas* are:

1. *Rig-veda*
2. *Yajur-veda*
3. *Sama-veda*
4. *Atharva-veda*

The *Rig-veda* was first a monotone chant (*archika gana*), then a two-toned (*gathika*) and eventually a three-toned chant (*samika*). In the *samika*, there was one main tone (*svarita*) and two accents, one higher (*udatta*) and one lower (*anudatta*). The accents were based on the requirement to emphasise certain portions of the text.

In the *Yajur-veda*, the chants evolved to two main tones and two accents forming a tetrachord. The *veena* is mentioned as an accompaniment to vocal recitations during the rituals.

The *Sama-veda* is the basis for Indian music. It added three more tones to the existing four, creating the full scale of seven notes. Within this scale were all the important and known musical intervals, and the concept of the octave is also mentioned.

The *Atharva-veda* is a collection of hymns and formulae. The hymns were recited with different notes during the performance of rites and rituals.

Upanishads

The *Upanishads*, also known as *Vedanta*, are considered the pinnacle of Vedic literature. In the *Upanishads*, the seven notes are discussed, as is the *adhara shadja* concept, where the Sa is kept constant, and all melodies can be sung with that as the tonic.

The Epics

The two great epics of India, the *Ramayana* and the *Mahabharata* reference *grama ragas*. In the *Ramayana*, poet Valmiki speaks of Lava and Kusa (sons of Lord Rama) singing in his court, and refers to *jaatis* and *moorchanas*, and instruments like the *veena* and the *mridangam*.

In music, theory generally follows practice. It is difficult to imagine a theoretical concept being developed before the practical application in any art form. For example, while developing the 72 *melakarta* system, Venkatamakhi based his classification of parent and derived scales on certain *ragas* that were practised and commonly used.

Dattilam is an ancient Indian musical text ascribed to the sage Dattila, and may predate the *Natyashastra* (because the *Natyashastra* references it). Written in 244 verses, *Dattilam* marks the transition from the *Sama-gana*—i.e., ritual *Sama-vedic* recitation—to *Gandharva* music.

Dattilam expounds concepts of *swara*, *sthana*, *moorchana*, *alankara*, *tanas* and *grama* which contain twenty-two microtones or *sruti*s in an octave. The melodic structure consists of eighteen groups called *jaatis*, which predates the *raga* system.

Bharata Muni's **Natyashastra** is an early treatise on drama, dance and music, and is an authoritative source of musicology. It speaks of twenty-two *srutis* (microtones), *moorchanas, jaatis, gramas* and the *audava/shadava*. There are also chapters on musical instruments, classifying them into *tata vadya* (stringed instruments), *avanaddha vadya* (instruments covered with stretched membrane or skin), *ghana vadya* (solid instruments) and *susira vadya* (wind instruments). This is very similar to a classification published in the West in the early 1900s.

Matanga Muni's fifth-century **Brihaddesi** is another important music treatise. Besides covering topics like *gramas* and *jaatis*, dealt with in the *Natyashastra*, Matanga also talks about the *raga*, which had taken the place of the *jaatis*, and states that the *ragas* are known as *jaatis* because they were born of microtones or *srutis*, initial notes or *grahas*, and clusters of tones. Or, because the realisation of aesthetic sentiments is possible from them, they are known as *jaatis*.

Dravidian Music

Simultaneous but independently, at this time, Dravidian music was also developing. Dravidian music's nomenclature is different from that of the Sanskrit treatises, but the theory seems to be similar to that found in Bharata's *Natyashastra*. Ilango Adigal's **Silappadikaram** in Tamil, written between the second and fifth century CE contains some of the earliest expositions of the Indian musical scale. The seven notes were called *kural, tuttam, kaikkilai, uzhai, ili, vilari* and *taram*, and microtones were called *alagus*. *Panns* were parent scales and *tirams* were derived scales.

The Medieval Period

Jayadeva's twelfth-century **Gita Govinda** was a monumental work of the medieval period. The *Gita Govinda* was the first to set melody and rhythm together in a uniform pattern, known as *chhanda prabandha* (*chhanda* means metre and *prabandha* means composition). The *raga* and *tala* for each of the songs have been given, although the original tunes are no longer available to us. They are the earliest examples of regular musical compositions, and the *tala* of each composition is determined by the metre of the Sanskrit verse.

The work is divided into twelve chapters called *sargas* and consists of twenty-four songs called *ashtapadis*. Each song has eight sections (*ashta* meaning eight; *pada* meaning line). *Gita Govinda* is of both religious and musical significance, and the *ashtapadis* are sung all over India since they were written before Indian music split into the two systems.

Sarngadeva (1210–1247 CE), in the **Sangeeta Ratnakara**, classified *ragas* according to the seasons and times of the day, and discussed the techniques of playing *ragas* in different ways, the feeling of the melodies, the importance of certain notes (*vadi* and *samvadi*), the grace notes and other embellishments. He spoke of *bhava* (emotion) and explored different aspects of rhythm.

The division of Indian classical music into South Indian or Carnatic and North Indian or Hindustani music during the thirteenth century CE was a major milestone, as until that time, Indian music was believed to be homogeneous throughout the country. In the North, the music was subjected to Arab and Persian influences and began to change. The South remained relatively uninfluenced since the invaders did not establish rule south of the Vindhyas. This eventually brought about the development of the two distinct systems.

Development of Carnatic Music

As Hindustani music began to change, Carnatic music continued to develop along the same path as before.

Sri Vidyaranya (1320–1380 CE), one of the Shankaracharyas and the founder of the Vijayanagara Empire, used the term *mela* for derived (*janaka*) *raga*s in his treatise **Sangeeta Sudha**. He has mentioned fifteen *mela*s and fifty *janya raga*s, and the concept of sixteen *swara*s in an octave.

Annamacharya (1424–1503 CE) was the eldest member of a family of composers from Tallapakam and a great devotee of Lord Venkateshwara. The Tallapakkam composers were some of the first to compose in the *kriti* form with three sections, *pallavi*, *anupallavi* and *charanam*. He is believed to have composed 30,000 songs, both in Sanskrit and Telugu.

Purandara Dasa (1484–1564 CE) is known as *Karnataka Sangeeta Pitamaha* (the grandfather of Carnatic music). A prolific composer, he laid the foundation for present-day Carnatic music. He brought about a major transformation insofar as he tried to systematically devise a method for learning South Indian music. He created scale exercises (*sarale varase*) and exercises to expand the vocal range (*tara sthayi* and *mandra sthayi varase*). He also created *gitams*, simple melodic compositions in a particular *raga*, set to a rhythmic cycle where each syllable is set to a particular note.

Swaramelakalanidhi authored by Ramamatya was

published in 1550 CE. It is considered to be one of the most important works tracing the history of the modern period. Ramamatya discarded the *grama-moorchana-jaati* system describing the *mela raga* in clear, precise terms. He was the first to clearly classify *raga*s into a system of parent (*janaka*) and derived (*janya*) *raga*s. Venkatamakhi later built his classic scheme of the seventy-two *melakartas* on this. Ramamatya mentions twenty *melas* and sixty-four *janya raga*s along with their *swaras*. In fact, he uses the term *mela* in the title of the *grantha* highlighting its importance.

Narayana Teertha (1580–1660 CE) was the author of the *Sri Krishna Lila Tarangini*, a Sanskrit dance drama.

The Modern Period

During the seventeenth century, Lochana in his treatise **Raga Tarangini** mentioned twelve *thaats* (*melas*) and seventy-eight *janya raga*s. He classified them on the basis of *shuddha, komala* and *tivra swaras*.

Somanatha (1609 CE), in his treatise **Raga Vibodha**, mentioned 960 *melas* derived from seven *shuddha swaras* and fifteen *vikrita swaras*. He further explained that only twenty-three *melas* were in vogue during his period, and also gave the characteristics of the *melas* like *graha, amsha, nyasa* and time of rendering.

Kshetragna (1600–1680 CE) was a contemporary of Venkatamakhi. He is credited with perfecting the compositional style of the *padam*. He composed over 4,100 *padams*, several of them in rare *ragas*. The *padams* dealt with the themes of longing for the Lord, pangs of separation, jealousy and betrayal, using the *nayaka–nayaki* approach of Jayadeva.

Ventakamakhi wrote the ***Chaturdandi Prakasika***, published around 1660 CE. This work is the basis of the present-day system of music, and deals with *sruti*s (microtones), *swaras* (notes), *ragas*, *talas* and *melas*. His most significant contribution to Carnatic music is the formulation of the scheme of the seventy-two *melakartas* (parent scales). He worked it out scientifically applying the process of permutation and combination on the twelve notes on a scale. Venkatamakhi classified the *melas* but the process of naming the seventy-two was completed by his grandson Muddu Venkatamakhi.

Tulaja, the king of Thanjavur who ruled during the eighteenth century, wrote on *melas* in his grantha ***Sangeeta Saramrita***. Along with Venkatamakhi's *melas*, he listed out nineteen *melas* that were in vogue during his days.

On the basis of Venkatamakhi's seventy-two *melas*, Govindacharya, author of ***Sangraha Choodamani***, outlined some more rules and formulated *melas*. It is Govindacharya's classification that is being followed today.

The Golden Age of Carnatic Music

The eighteenth century is considered as the golden age of Carnatic music. During this time lived three great composers/musicians who were later celebrated as the musical trinity: Shyama Shastri, Tyagaraja and Muthuswami Dikshitar. Their knowledge, deep spirituality, profound musicianship, creativity and innovations make their contribution to Carnatic music invaluable.

Shyama Shastri (1762–1827 CE), one among the musical trinity, was responsible for many great compositions. He also composed *navarathnamalika*, a group of nine *kriti*s for goddess Meenakshi of Madurai. He used different *tala*s but was a specialist in *Mishra chapu tala*. His *mudra* (or signature word) was Shyamakrishna.

Tyagaraja (1767–1847 CE) was a prolific composer, who composed over 24,000 compositions. They were mostly in Telugu and a few were in Sanskrit. He is credited with evolving and perfecting the *kriti* form. The concept of the *sangati* (melodic variations on a line in the composition used to beautify it) was his contribution. His *pancharatna kriti*s form an important part of Carnatic music repertoire even today. His *mudra* was Tyagaraja.

Muthuswami Dikshitar (1775–1835 CE) was a composer who sang *kriti*s in praise of all deities. His songs are normally slow in tempo and bring out the depth and beauty of a *raga*. His *mudra* was *guruguha*. During this period, when the British were ruling India, many Western bands performed for the East India Company at Fort St. George (Madras). This resulted in Muthuswami Dikshitar's brother, Baluswami Dikshitar, introducing the present form of the violin (which was used by the Westerners) into Indian music. This brought in a major change, and the violin eventually became an important accompanying instrument for singers, replacing other accompanying instruments.

Moreover, Muthuswami Dikshitar, during his stay in Varanasi (with his spiritual *guru* Chidambaranatha Yogi), was exposed to a lot of North Indian music, including the Dhrupad style. Being a visionary with a broad mind, he was influenced by it and it reflects in his compositions which are comparatively slow paced. He also introduced some North Indian *raga*s into

South Indian music and made compositions (for example, the *kriti* Akhilandeshwari in *Raga* Dwijavanti). Dikshitar—during the early part of his life, because of the influence of his family patron, Venkatakrishna Mudaliyar, was exposed to Western music—adapted Western melodies, and created '*nottuswarams*' using Sanskrit text. Even though Western and North Indian influences were evident, he still retained the identity of South Indian classical music, in a way, creating even heavier South Indian classical compositions, still fusing Western and North Indian concepts together. This puts him in a special position as the first fusion artist and composer of India.

Maharaja Svati Tirunal (1813–1847 CE), the king of Travancore, now Kerala, composed over 400 songs. He composed *swarajati*s, *varnam*s, *padam*s, *javali*s and musical dramas. He also composed *dhrupad*s, *khyal bandish*es, *tappa*s, *thumri*s and *bhajan*s in the Hindustani style. He used the *mudra* 'Padmanabha' and its synonyms.

Maha Vaidyanatha Iyer (1844–1893 CE) was a brilliant composer who created *varnam*s, *kriti*s and *tillana*s. His unique *tillana* in *raga* Kaanada is set to Simhanandana *tala*. He also composed a *ragamalika* on the seventy-two *melakarta*s. He used the *mudra* Guhadasa in his compositions.

Patnam Subramanya Iyer (1845–1902 CE) was a great composer and performer, who belonged to the *shishya parampara* of Tyagaraja. His compositions include *kriti*s, *tana varnam*s, *pada varnam*s, *javali*s and *tillana*s.

Harikesanallur Mutthaiah Bhagavathar (1877–1945 CE) was a composer who composed in Sanskrit, Telugu, Tamil and Kannada. He composed *varnam*s, *kriti*s, *tillana*s and *ragamalika*s, using the *mudra* 'Harikesa'. He did much to popularise Svati Tirunal's compositions. He invented many new *ragas* as well.

Koteeswara Iyer (1869–1938 CE) was one of the first composers to compose in all seventy-two *melakarta ragas*. He was the grandson of Kavi Kunjara Bharathi, and took the *mudra* Kavi Kunjara Dasan in his honour.

Veena Shivaramaiah (1886–1946 CE) of Mysore too composed *kriti*s in all the seventy-two *melakarta*s as per the wishes of King Nalwadi Krishnaraja Wodeyar.

Belakawadi Srinivasa Iyengar (1888–1936 CE), one of the court musicians of Mysore, composed *kriti*s in seventy-two *melakarta ragas* as per the wishes of his patron Nalwadi Krishnaraja Wodeyar. He played two *kriti*s every day on violin and showed the intricacies of the *ragas* to the king.

Papanasam Sivan (1890–1973 CE) composed over 2,500 songs in many different *ragas* in Tamil and Sanskrit. He composed for and performed in theatrical productions, and taught at Kalakshetra. From 1935 CE onwards, he composed for and even acted in films.

Post-Independence Period

Carnatic music is a living style of music and continues to develop, adapt and evolve. In addition to examining the development and history of Carnatic music, it is useful to understand its current structure.

A clearer understanding of the development of the *raga* system will be presented in the next chapter, but right now, it is sufficient for the reader to know that the present Carnatic melodic system is based on the *melakarta* concept with seventy-two *melakarta* or *janaka* (parent) scales and thousands of *janya* or derived scales.

Talas

The *Tala* system in Carnatic music is sophisticated and has been methodically developed. The *tala* system is a group of rhythmic cycles. Each composition is usually based on a particular *tala*. The current system in use is of seven basic *talas*, which can be expanded to a system of thirty-five *talas*.

There are three components or parts, which make up the seven *talas*. (There are actually six components, but only three are widely used.) These components are known as *angas* (literally 'limbs'), and a *tala* can have one, two or all three. The *angas* are: *Laghu*, *Drutam* and *Anudrutam*. The *laghu* is a necessity in every *tala*, and the number of beats can be three, four, five, seven or nine. This number is known as the *jaati*.

Table 2: *Jaatis*

Jaati name	No. of beats in a *laghu*
Trishra	3
Chaturashra	4
Khanda	5
Mishra	7
Sankeerna	9

If no number is indicated next to the *laghu*, it is assumed to be four beats. The *drutam* is always two beats and the *anudrutam* is one beat.

Table 3: *Tala* Components

Tala	Components
Dhruva	1 *laghu*, 1 *drutam*, 2 *laghus*
Matya	1 *laghu*, 1 *drutam*, 1 *laghu*
Rupaka	1 *drutam*, 1 *laghu*
Jhampa	1 *laghu*, 1 *anudrutam*, 1 *drutam*
Triputa	1 *laghu*, 2 *drutams*
Ata	2 *laghus*, 2 *drutams*
Eka	1 *laghu*

The number of beats in a *laghu* is variable. If variations of each of the seven basic *tala*s are constructed using different *laghus*, the system is expanded to thirty-five different *tala*s.

If a *tala* has more than one *laghu*, the number of beats (or *jaati*) must remain the same for all of them.

Additionally, each beat can be further divided into a number of *nadai*s, or pulses per beat—again, three, four, five, seven or nine. This further expands the system of 35 *tala*s to 175 *tala*s.

There is another system of *tala*s in use. It is known as *chapu tala*s. They are syncopated rhythmic cycles. The four *chapu tala*s are *Trishra chapu* (three beats), *Khanda chapu* (five beats), *Mishra chapu* (seven beats) and *Sankeerna chapu* (nine beats).

Compositional Forms

Compositional forms in Carnatic music are divided into two groups: *Abhyasa gana* (practice songs) and *Sabha gana* (songs for audiences). *Abhyasa gana* has been devised for instruction and learning, for one to practise and learn technical skills, while *sabha gana* is for public performance.

Abhyasa gana forms include *gitams*, *swarajatis*, *jatiswarams* and *varnams*. *Gitams* are simple songs and are often the first compositions learnt. *Gitams* usually have simple metre and are set to a particular *raga* and *tala*. *Lakshana gitams* are a particular type of *gitam* where the lyric describes the attributes of the *raga* it is composed in.

Swarajatis are compositions with three parts: *pallavi*, *anupallavi* and *charanam*. *Jatiswarams* are similar to *swarajatis* in terms of composition, but *jatiswarams* are primarily used as dance accompaniments.

Varnams are the most important and complex forms of *abhyasa gana* and are at times also performed as the first composition in concerts. A *varnam* is divided into two parts: the first part has the *pallavi*, *anupallavi* and *chitta swaras*, and the second part has the *charanam*, which is a melodic point of return, and *charana swaras* or *ettugada swaras*.

Sabha gana forms include *kritis*, *padams*, *javalis*, *tillanas* and *ragam-tanam-pallavi*.

Kritis are the most important forms of the *abhyasa gana* group, and the most commonly performed type of compositions performed in a concert. Like the other compositional forms discussed above, a *kriti* is set in a particular *raga*, and set to a specified *tala*. A *kriti* has three parts: the *pallavi*, the *anupallavi* and the *charanam*. Each part has a melody, which is repeated with variations known as *sangatis*. *Padams* and *tillanas* are compositional forms commonly used for dance, and *javali*s are compositions which are 'lighter' and deal with more temporal themes, and have lyrics that are often colloquial.

Most music in the Carnatic tradition is spiritual and in praise of a God or Goddess. Music is believed to be of divine origin, and a means of enlightenment.

Instruments in Carnatic Music

Instruments used commonly in Carnatic music can be divided into stringed instruments (or *tata vadya*), wind instruments (also called aerophones or *susira vadya*) and percussion instruments. Percussion instruments are classified into hollow instruments (membranophones or *avanaddha vadya*) and solid instruments (idiophones or *ghana vadya*).

Stringed instruments include the *tambura, veena, gottuvadyam* and violin. Wind instruments include the *nadaswaram, ottu* and bamboo flute. Percussion instruments include the *mridangam, tavil* and *kanjira* in the membranophone category, and *ghatam, morsing, jalra* and *jalatarang* in the idiophone category.

Some of the instruments that were earlier used more as accompanying instruments have gained prominence and have developed into solo instruments. An example of this is the violin. It is interesting to note that the violin that is at present used in Indian music was first adapted to Carnatic music during the British period. Similarly, in recent years, many Western instruments like the guitar, mandolin and saxophone have been successfully introduced and adapted.

Around the first half of this century, some Hindustani classical musicians and musicologists started taking an interest in, and tried to understand, the extremely complex nature of the rhythmic structure and the melodic concept of Carnatic music. Some of the *ragas* of the South were also adapted and performed by them. However, the adaptation of Hindustani *ragas* into the Carnatic system had started much earlier, more than a century ago. During his time, the great composer Muthuswami Dikshitar travelled in the North and composed songs based on several Hindustani *ragas*. Even today, it is not uncommon to hear a bhajan (a Hindustani musical form) performed in a Carnatic music concert.

Another recent development has been the emergence of Carnatic–Hindustani *jugalbandi* (*jugalbandi* means 'duet'). *Jugalbandi* was normally a duet between two musicians, vocal or instrumental. This was more common amongst brothers or musicians who were students of the same *guru* and belonged to the same style of music. This is not necessarily like that now. There are *jugalbandi*s between various artists of different styles using unusual combinations of instruments. In a Carnatic–Hindustani *jugalbandi,* as the name implies, two artists, one from each tradition, come together to perform. There have been occasions where a Hindustani percussionist has accompanied a Carnatic performer (together with one or more Carnatic accompanists) and vice versa. Some of these novelties have been successful. Also, the concept of the percussion ensemble (*tala vadya*), which is a part of the Southern tradition, has been adapted in the North using both North and South Indian percussion instruments. Similarly, *konnakkol* (using the voice as a percussion instrument by reciting percussive syllables in a music performance) a practice in the Carnatic tradition, has also been adapted in the North.

3

Raga and *Mela* in Carnatic Music

The development of the concepts of the *raga* and the *mela* is essentially the history of Carnatic music. While tracing the evolution of these two concepts, it is useful and necessary to refer to *lakshanagrantha*s or treatises that have been written on music over the centuries.

Evolution of the *Raga*

A *swara* can be described as *a delightful sound which is infinite and emerges from the microtones.* It can be called a developed *sruti.* The term *sruti* refers to musical intervals or microtones which make up a *saptaka* (octave). It is derived from the Sanskrit root (*dhaatu*) 'sru' meaning 'to hear'. It is the smallest audible difference of pitch and also the smallest fraction of a semitone. It is defined as *the minutest difference in pitch that can be distinguished by the human ear.* It is a fundamental aspect of Indian music, especially applicable to the *raga* concept. It beautifies the *raga* and certain *sruti*s gain the status of a *swara* in certain *raga*s.

Many milestones can be traced in the development of the *raga* over the centuries.

Grama–Moorchana–Jaati System

*Grama*s are a group of *swara*s in an octave, just like a group of orderly houses in a village.

Bharata's *Natyashastra* states that *moorchana*s are scales (like present-day *mela*s) and when *lakshana*s or characteristics are added, they evolve into *jaati*s (later called *raga*s). It names the following *moorchana*s as a part of the *shadja grama mandala* and *madhyama grama mandala*. The *gandhara grama mandala* was obsolete long before Bharata's period. (See Table 4.)

Table 4: *Grama–Moorchana–Jaati* system

Swaras	Name of the *Moorchana*
Shadja grama mandala	
S R G M P D N	Uttaramandra
Ṇ S R G M P D	Rajani
Ḍ Ṇ S R G M P	Uttarayata
Ṗ Ḍ Ṇ S R G M	Shuddha Shadja
Ṃ Ṗ Ḍ Ṇ S R G	Matsarikrita
Ġ Ṃ Ṗ Ḍ Ṇ S R	Ashvakranta
Ṛ Ġ Ṃ Ṗ Ḍ Ṇ S	Abhirudgata

Madhyama grama mandala	
M P D N Ṡ Ṙ Ġ	Souviri
G M P D N Ṡ Ṙ	Harinashva
R G M P D N Ṡ	Kalopanata
S R G M P D N	Shuddhamadhya
Ṇ S R G M P D	Maargi
Ḍ Ṇ S R G M P	Pouravi
Ṗ Ḍ Ṇ S R G M	Hrishyaka

Gramas are the sources of the *moorchanas*. By a modal shift of tonic, *sruti bheda* or *graha bheda*, a group of seven scales called *moorchanas* were derived. From the two *gramas—shadja* and *madhyama*—fourteen *moorchanas*, seven from each *grama*, were evolved. Among the fourteen, some *moorchanas* are repeated and only seven *moorchanas* remain. These *moorchanas* evolve into *jaatis*, which are termed *shuddha jaatis*—four from the *shadja grama* called *Shaadji, Naishadi, Dhaivati* and *Aarshabhi,* and three from the *madhyama grama* called *Gandhari, Madhyama* and *Panchami* respectively.

Moorchanas were classified into: *Audava* or *Audavita*, which have five *swaras* in *Aarohana* and *Avarohana*; *Shadava*, which have six *swaras* in *Aarohana* and *Avarohana*; and *Sampoorna*, which have seven *swaras* in *Aarohana* and *Avarohana*.

These combinations evolved into eighteen *jaatis*—seven from *shadja grama* and eleven from *madhyama grama* (see Table 5). Some were *shuddha jaatis* and some *vikrita jaatis* (those with *mishra* of more than one *jaati*).

Table 5: Descriptions of *Jaatis*

Number	Jaati	Description
1.	Shaadji	*Shuddha Jaati* with *Shadja swara* being *Graha* and *Amsha*
2.	Aarshabhi	*Shuddha Jaati* with *Rishabha swara* being *Graha* and *Amsha*
3.	Gandhari	*Shuddha Jaati* with *Gandhara swara* being *Graha* and *Amsha*
4.	Madhyama	*Shuddha Jaati* with *Madhyama swara* being *Graha* and *Amsha*
5.	Panchami	*Shuddha Jaati* with *Panchama swara* being *Graha* and *Amsha*
6.	Dhaivati	*Shuddha Jaati* with *Dhaivata swara* being *Graha* and *Amsha*
7.	Naishadi	*Shuddha Jaati* with *Nishada swara* being *Graha* and *Amsha*
8.	Shadja Kaishiki	*Vikrita jaati*; a combination of Shaadji and Gandhari *jaatis*
9.	Shadjodichyava	*Vikrita jaati*; a combination of Shaadji, Gandhari Dhaivati *jaatis*
10.	Shadja madhyama	*Vikrita jaati*; a combination of Shaadji and Madhyama *jaatis*
11.	Gandharodichyava	*Vikrita jaati*; a combination of Gandhari, Dhaivati, Shaadji and Madhyama *jaatis*
12.	Raktagandhari	*Vikrita jaati*; a combination of Gandhari, Naishadi, Panchami and Madhyama

13.	Kaishiki	*Vikrita jaati*; a combination of Shaadji, Gandhari, Madhyama, Panchami and Naishadi *jaatis*
14.	Madhyamodichyava	*Vikrita jaati*; a combination of Gandhari, Dhaivati, Panchami and Madhyama *jaatis*
15.	Kaarmaaravi	*Vikrita jaati*; a combination of Naishadi, Aarshabhi and Panchami *jaatis*
16.	Gandhara Panchami	*Vikrita jaati*; a combination of Gandhari and Panchami *jaatis*
17.	Aandhri	*Vikrita jaati*; a combination of Gandhari and Aarshabhi *jaatis*
18.	Nandayanti	*Vikrita jaati*; a combination of Aarshabhi, Gandhari and Panchami *jaatis*

Gradually, only *shadja grama* was in vogue and all the *jaatis* (*ragas*) were accepted to be born out of the *graha bheda* (modal shift of the tonic) of *shadja grama*.

Matanga has defined *raga* in the sense of a melody. He interpreted *jaati* as *raga*. He described *raga* as a group of luminous notes with an integrated discipline of *sruti* relationship, a power to evoke sentiment. Thus *jaati* was the genus for the *raga*.

Narada's **Sangeeta Makaranda**, composed in twelfth century CE, recognised *jaati*s as full-fledged *ragas* and was the first to classify *ragas* in male and female forms (*ragas* and *raginis*) and *putra ragas*.

Swami Prajnanananda writes, 'The *jaatis* were the *ragas* by themselves, as they used to create a pleasing and soothing sensation in the heart of living beings.'

1. *Amsha*—predominant note
2. *Graha*—the initial note
3. *Tara*—the higher octave note
4. *Mandra*—the lower octave note
5. *Nyasa*—the final note
6. *Apanyasa*—the secondary final note
7. *Alpatva*—a rarely used note, of which there are two types: *langhana*, which is just a slight touch or omission of the *swara*, and the *anabhyasa* where the *swara* is used sparingly
8. *Bahutva*—the amplification or prevalence of a *swara*
9. *Shadava*—the hexatonic treatment of *swaras* by the elimination of one *swara* from the seven notes
10. *Audava*—pentatonic use of *swaras*

After the *jaati*s, the next form to take shape in the evolution of the *raga* concept was the *grama raga*, which evolved from the *jaati*s. *Grama raga*s are of two kinds, namely *shuddha* and *vikrita*.

Shuddha–Chayalaga–Sankeerna

Matanga classified *raga*s as *Shuddha–Chayalaga–Sankeerna* in his **Brihaddeshi**. According to this classification, *Shuddha ragas* are those which have 'pure notes', that is, notes which do not have traces of any other notes, with totally independent characteristics and *raga bhava*. This later paved the way for *melakartas*.

Chayalaga (also called *Saalaga* or *Saalanka*) refers to *raga*s that have a foreign note or take another note from a different *raga*. These *ragas* occasionally give the tonality of another *raga*.

Sankeerna (also called *Mishra* or *Sankrama*) has tonalities of more than two *ragas*.

Raganga–Upanga–Bhashanga–Kriyanga

Parshvadeva of twelfth century CE, in his *Sangeeta Samayasaara*, classified *ragas* as *Raganga*, *Upanga*, *Bhashanga* and *Kriyanga*. By combining each of these with *Sampoorna*, *Shadava* and *Audava*, he presented the twelve sets listed in Table 6:

Table 6: *Raganga—Upanga—Bhashanga—Kriyanga*

	Raganga	**Upanga**	**Bhashanga**	**Kriyanga**
Sampoorna	*Raganga Sampoorna*	*Upanga Sampoorna*	*Bhashanga Sampoorna*	*Kriyanga Sampoorna*
Shadava	*Raganga Shadava*	*Upanga Shadava*	*Bhashanga Shadava*	*Kriyanga Shadava*
Audava	*Raganga Audava*	*Upanga Audava*	*Bhashanga Audava*	*Kriyanga Audava*

Narada's classifications in *Sangeeta Makaranda*

In the **Sangeeta Makaranda** of Narada emerged the classification of *purusha-sthree-napunsaka ragas; muktanga kampita-ardha kampita-kampaviheena,* on the basis of *gamakas*; early morning, morning, afternoon, evening and night *ragas*; *raga* (male), *ragini* (female) and their *putra* (progeny).

Marga and Deshi Ragas

Marga ragas are the *ragas* born from *jaatis*. These *ragas* strictly adhere to rules. *Deshi ragas*, on the other hand, are those that have undergone changes over the years. Only some rules from *Marga ragas* were followed in *Deshi ragas*.

Uttama–Madhyama–Adhama

This classification was mentioned by Ramamatya in *Swara Mela Kalanidhi* followed by Somanatha in his *Raga Vibodha*. *Shuddha ragas*, which had independent characteristics without taking the shades of any other *ragas*, were called *Uttama ragas*. These *ragas* were believed to be ideal for detailed elaboration of the *raga* and the *tana*, and appropriate for composing. These were very popular *ragas*.

Madhyama ragas were basic in their characteristics and very few types of compositions could be composed in them. These *ragas* were rare.

Adhama ragas were not suitable for scholarly compositions.

Evolution of the *Melas*

Vidyaranya (1268–1386 CE), the author of **Sangeeta Saara**, was the first to use the term *mela* to denote a parent *raga*. Classification of *ragas* in Carnatic music began with the scheme of *Mela* and *Janya ragas*. Vidyaranya developed a system of fifteen *melas*, and they were named as follows: Natta, Gurjari, Varatika, Sri-raga, Bhairavi, Shankarabharana, Ahiri, Vasantabhairavi, Samanta, Kambodhi, Mukhari, Shuddharamakriya, Kedaragowla, Hejjujji and Deshakshi. He also dealt with fifty derived *ragas*. It is interesting to note that the order of these *melas* is not in any logical sequence.

Ramamatya's **Swaramelakalanidhi** was based on Sarngadeva's *Sangeeta Ratnakara*, and was published in 1550 CE. This was the first work to use the word *mela* in its title. Ramamatya proposed five *vikruta swaras*, for a total of twelve *swaras* in an octave. Ramamatya is known as the 'father of the *Mela* concept', as he was the first to have a separate chapter on *melas*, known as *Mela Prakarana*. He provided a list of twenty *melas* and sixty-four *janya ragas*, where *Shadja* and *Panchama* were fixed notes. The *melas* listed by him are those that were in use at the time of his writing.

The *melas* according to Ramamatya were: Mukhari, Malavagowla, Sriraga, Saranganata, Hindola, Shuddharamakriya, Deshakshi, Kannadagowla, Shuddhanati, Ahari, Nadaramakriya, Shuddhavarali, Reetigowla, Vasanthabhairavi, Kedaragowla, Hejjujji, Samavarali, Revagupti, Samanta and Kambhoji.

This list of *melas* and *janyas* has been considerably expanded over time, and many of Ramamatya's *melas* are now considered *janya ragas*. Ramamatya clearly explained concepts like *mela* and *raga*, with the *madhya sthayi shadja* as the common fundamental note.

In the latter part of the sixteenth century, Pundarika Vittala proposed a system of ninety *melas* in **Sadragachandrodaya**. The classification is based on twelve notes in an octave and seventeen possible denominations. This work is the first example of a logical arrangement of *melas*.

Raga Vibodha, produced in 1609 CE by Somanatha, was inspired by Ramamatya's **Swaramelakalanidhi**, but was far more advanced with respect to *swara*, *sruti*, *mela* and *raga*.

Raga Vibodha contains five chapters or *viveka*s, and in the chapter called *Mela Viveka, mela* is defined as a 'harmonious combination of *swaras*'. Somanatha mentions fourteen *swaras* in an octave, seven *shuddha swaras* and seven *vikruta swaras*. With these *swaras*, he propounds 960 possible *mela* combinations. But the following twenty-three *melas* were in vogue during his period: Mukhari, Revagupti, Samavarali, Todi, Ramakriya, Bhairava, Vasantha, Vasanthabhairavi, Malavagowla, Reetigowla, Abhira, Hammira, Shuddhavarati, Shuddharamakri, Sriraga, Kalyana, Kambhoji, Mallari, Samanta, Karnatakagowla, Deshakshi, Shuddhanata and Saranga.

This work envisaged particular deities for *ragas*, including their colour, dress, features and seasons.

Sangeeta Sudha is a seventeenth-century work by Govinda Dikshitar, which presents an in-depth discussion on the styles and systems of music present at the time of its being written. It discusses 264 *ragas* and the *lakshanas* for about fifty *ragas*. This work also provides insight into the **Sangeeta Sara** of Vidyaranya.

Venkatamakhi's seminal work, the **Chaturdandiprakashika**, written in 1650 CE, had a profound influence on every musician that came after him. The nineteen *melas* in use during his time were: Mukhari, Samavarali, Bhupala, Hejjujji, Vasantabhairavi, Gowla, Bhairavi, Ahari, Sriraga, Kambhoji, Shankarabharana, Samanta, Deshakshi, Nata, Shuddhavarali, Panthuvarali, Shuddharamakriya, Simharava (created by Venkatamakhi) and Kalyani.*

---

* Veṅkaṭamakhi and R. Sathyanarayana. *Caturdaṇḍīprakāśikā*. New Delhi: Indira Gandhi National Centre for the Arts in association with Motilal Banarsidass Publishers, Delhi, 2002. p. 187.

Though in his formulation, Venkatamakhi laid the foundation for the seventy-two mela system, he only described nineteen of them. The names for all of them were given by his grandson, Muddu Venkatamakhi, who also composed *lakshana geetas* in each, and published them in his work *Ragalakshanam*.

The *melakarta* concept uses the twelve semitones, enharmonically divided into sixteen notes:

Table 7: Sixteen Note System of Carnatic Music

Name	Note	Interval
Shadja	S	(tonic)
Shuddha Rishabha	R_1	Minor second
Chatusruti Rishabha	R_2	Major second
Shatsruti Rishabha	R_3	Augmented second
Shuddha Gandhara	G_1	Diminished third
Sadharana Gandhara	G_2	Minor third
Antara Gandhara	G_3	Major third
Shuddha Madhyama	M_1	Perfect fourth
Prati Madhyama	M_2	Augmented fourth
Panchama	P	Perfect fifth
Shuddha Dhaivata	D_1	Minor sixth
Chatusruti Dhaivata	D_2	Major sixth
Shatsruti Dhaivata	D_3	Augmented sixth
Shuddha Nishada	N_1	Diminished seventh
Kaishiki Nishada	N_2	Minor seventh
Kakali Nishada	N_3	Major seventh

As can be seen from Table 7, the following are enharmonic equivalents (see Table 8):

Table 8: Enharmonic Equivalents

$R_2 = G_1$
$R_3 = G_2$
$D_2 = N_1$
$D_3 = N_2$

The *mela or melakarta ragas* are created by using combinations of the notes in Table 7.[*]

Of the seventy-two *melakartas*, the first thirty-six are very similar to the second thirty-six with the only difference being that the first thirty-six use a perfect fourth (*shuddha madhyama*) and the second thirty-six use an augmented fourth (*prati madhyama*). Each group of thirty-six *ragas* is further divided into groups of six known as *chakras*. In each *chakra*, the first tetra chord is the same, and the second tetra chord changes by one note.

Bhutasankhya

Since ancient times, the *Bhutasankhya* system was popular in India, especially among mathematicians and astronomers. This was the concept of using Sanskrit words to denote numerical values associated with them. This system was used to name the *chakras* and the *ragas* within the *chakras* as follows:

---

[*] L. Subramaniam and Viji Subramaniam, *Euphony*, New Delhi: Affiliated East-West Press, 1995, p. 42.

Table 9: *Bhutasankhya*

Chakra	Name	Meaning	Details
I	Indu	1 Moon	
II	Netra	2 Eyes	
III	Agni	3 Types of fire	Dakshina, Aavaahaneeya, Garhapathya
IV	Veda	4 Vedas	Rig, Yajur, Sama, Atharva
V	Baana	5 Arrows of Manmatha	Lotus, Mango, Ashoka, Jasmine and Blue Water Lily flowers
VI	Ritu	6 Seasons	Vasanta, Greeshma, Varsha, Sharad, Hemanta and Shishira
VII	Rishi	7 Sages	Gautama, Bharadwaja, Vishwamitra, Jamdagni, Vasishta, Kashyapa, Atri
VIII	Vasu	8 Attenders of Indra	Dhara (Earth), Anala (Fire), Apa (Water), Anila (Wind), Dhruva (North Star), Soma (Moon), Prabhasa (Dawn) and Pratyusha (Light)
IX	Brahma	9 Prajapatis (deities presiding over protection of life)	Angiras, Atri, Kashyapa, Pulastya, Pulaha, Bhrigu, Marichi, Vasishta, Daksha
X	Dishi	10 Directions	Uttara (north), Dakshina (south), Purva (east), Paschima (west), Agneya (south-east), Nairutya (south-west), Vayuvya (north-west), Eeshanya (north-east), Akasha (sky), Patala (netherworld)

XI	Rudra	11 Gods of destruction	Mahadeva, Shiva, Rudra, Shankara, Nilalohita, Ishana, Vijaya, Bhima, Devadeva, Bhava, Kapali
XII	Aditya	12 Gods of preservation	Amsha, Aryaman, Bhaga, Daksha, Mitra, Pusan, Sakra, Savitr, Tvastar, Varuna, Vishnu, Vivasvat

Katapayadi Sutra

The *Katapayadi* system was first seen in 683 CE, in Haridatta's **Grahachaaranibandhana**. The system was based on substituting letters for numerals to make them memorable, and has been applied to both the *Asampoorna* and *Sampoorna mela* systems, as well as to *suladi tala*s.

Numbers correspond to sounds in the following way:

Table 10: *Katapayadi Sutra*

Number	Sounds
1	ka, ta, pa, ya
2	kha, tta, fa, ra
3	ga, da, ba, la
4	gha, dda, bha, va
5	gna, nna, ma, sha
6	cha, tha, ssha
7	chha, thha, sa
8	ja, da, ha
9	jha, dhha,
0	jna, na

By taking the corresponding numbers of the first two consonants of a *raga* name, and reversing those numbers, one can derive the *mela* number.

The seventy-two *raga*s according to this *asampoorna mela paddhati* are shown on the next page (Table 11).

Venkatamakhi's classification inspired many other scholars, including Hindustani musicologist V.N. Bhatkande who wanted 'rules of *raga*s to be fixed in North Indian music in a manner that they were fixed in South Indian music' and believed *Chaturdandiprakasika* would be central to the effort of restoring order to the then disordered state of Hindustani music.

Raga Tattva Vibodha by Srinivasa and **Sangeeta Parijatha** by Ahobala (both seventeenth century CE) highlighted the classification of *mela*s.

Meladhikari Lakshana (eighteenth century CE) spoke of 4,624 *mela*s derived from twenty-four *sruti*s. The author mentioned thirty-four *chakra*s and thirty-four *mela*s in each *chakra*, using four *madhyama*s (34x4 = 136 *chakra*s x 34 = 4,624).

Table 11: Seventy-two *ragas* according to *asampoorna mela paddhati*

Chakra Name	Scale	Ascending	Descending	Asampoorna Mela
I *Indu*	1	$S R_1 M_1 P D_1 S$	$S N_1 D_1 P M_1 G_1 R_1 S$	*Kanakambari*
	2	$S R_1 M_1 P D_1 P N_2 S$	$S N_2 D_1 P M_1 G_1 R_1 S$	Phenadyuti
	3	$S R_1 M_1 P D_1 N_3 S$	$S N_3 D_1 P M_1 G_1 R_1 S$	Ganasamavarali
	4	$S R_1 M_1 P D_2 N_2 S$	$S N_2 D_2 P M_1 G_1 R_1 S$	Bhanumati
	5	$S R_1 M_1 P D_2 N_3 S$	$S N_3 D_2 P M_1 G_1 R_1 S$	Manoranjani
	6	$S R_1 M_1 P N_3 S$	$S N_3 D_3 N_3 P M_1 G_1 R_1 S$	Tanukirthi
II *Netra*	7	$S R_1 G_2 R_1 M_1 G_2 M_1 P N_1 D_1 S$	$S N_1 D_1 P M_1 G_2 M_1 G_2 R_1 S$	Senagrani
	8	$S R_1 G_2 M_1 P D_1 N_2 S$	$S N_2 D_1 M_1 P G_2 R_1 S$	Janatodi
	9	$S R_1 G_2 M_1 P D_1 N_3 S$	$S N_3 D_1 P M_1 G_2 R_1 S$	Dhunibhinnashadjam
	10	$S G_2 M_1 P N_2 D_2 N_2 S$	$S N_2 D_2 N_2 P N_2 P M_1 G_2 G_2 R_1 R_1 S$	Natabharanam
	11	$S R_1 G_2 M_1 P D_2 N_3 S$	$S N_3 D_2 P M_1 G_2 R_1 S$	Kokilaravam
	12	$S R_1 M_1 P S$	$S N_3 D_3 N_3 P M_1 G_2 S$	Rupavati

III *Agni*	13	$S R_1 M_1 G_3 M_1 P D_1 S$	$S N_1 D_1 P M_1 G_3 R_1 S$	Geyahejjajji
	14	$S R_1 G_3 M_1 P D_1 N_2 S$	$S N_2 D_1 M_1 G_3 M_1 P M_1 G_3 R_1 S$	Vativasantabhairavi
	15	$S R_1 G_3 M_1 P D_1 N_3 S$	$S N_3 D_1 P M_1 G_3 R_1 S$	Malavagaula
	16	$S R_1 G_3 M_1 P D_2 N_2 S$	$S N_2 D_2 P M_1 G_3 R_1 S$	Toyavegavahini
	17	$S R_1 G_3 M_1 D_2 N_3 S$	$S N_3 D_2 P M_1 G_3 R_1 S$	Chayavati
	18	$S R_1 G_3 M_1 P N_3 S$	$S N_3 D_3 N_3 P M_1 G_3 R_1 S$	Jayashuddhamalavi
IV *Veda*	19	$S R_2 G_2 M_1 P D_1 N_1 D_1 P D_1 S$	$S N_1 D_1 P M_1 G_2 R_2 G_2 R_2 S$	Jhankarabhramari
	20	$S G_2 R_2 G_2 M_1 N_2 D_1 M_1 N_2 N_2 S$	$S N_2 D_1 M_1 G_2 M_1 P M_1 G_2 R_2 S$	Naririigowla
	21	$S R_2 M_1 P D_1 P D_1 N_3 S$	$S N_3 P D_1 P M_1 P G_2 R_2 S$	Kiranavali
	22	$S R_2 M_1 P N_2 S$	$S N_2 P D_2 N_2 P M_1 R_2 G_2 R_2 S$	Shree
	23	$S R_2 G_2 S R_2 M_1 P D_2 S$	$S N_3 D_2 P M_1 G_2 R_2 S$	Gourivelavali
	24	$S R_2 M_1 P N_3 D_3 N_3 S$	$S N_3 P M_1 M_1 R_2 G_2 S$	Veeravasantam

Group	No.	Arohana	Avarohana	Name
V *Baana*	25	$S M_1 G_3 M_1 P D_1 N_1 D_1 S$	$S N_1 D_1 P M_1 G_3 R_2 S$	Sharavati
	26	$S R_2 G_3 P D_1 N_2 D_1 P D_1 S$	$S D_1 P G_3 R_2 S R_2 G_3 M_1 G_3 R_2 S$	Tarangini
	27	$S R_2 G_3 M_1 P D_1 N_3 S$	$S N_3 D_1 P M_1 G_3 R_2 G_3 S$	Sowrasena
	28	$S R_2 G_3 M_1 P D_2 N_2 S$	$S N_2 D_2 P M_1 G_3 R_2 S$	Harikedaragowla
	29	$S R_2 G_3 M_1 P D_2 N_3 S$	$S N_3 D_2 P M_1 G_3 R_2 S$	Dhirasankara-bharanam
	30	$S R_2 G_3 M_1 P N_3 D_3 N_3 S$	$S N_3 P M_1 G_3 R_2 S$	Nagabharanam
VI *Ritu*	31	$S R_3 G_3 M_1 P D_1 N_1 P D_1 S$	$S N_1 D_1 P M_1 R_3 G_3 M_1 R_3 S$	Kalavati
	32	$S M_1 R_3 G_3 M_1 P N_2 N_2 S$	$S N_2 D_1 P M_1 M_1 R_3 S$	Ragachudamani
	33	$S R_3 G_3 M_1 P D_1 N_3 S$	$S N_3 P D_1 M_1 M_1 G_3 M_1 R_3 S$	Gangatarangini
	34	$S R_3 G_3 M_1 P N_2 N_2 S$	$S N_2 D_2 N_2 P S N_2 P M_1 R_3 S$	Bhogachayanata
	35	$S M_1 G_3 P D_2 S$	$S N_3 D_2 S N_3 P M_1 R_3 S$	Shailadeshakshi
	36	$S R_3 G_3 M_1 P D_3 N_3 S$	$S N_3 P M_1 R_3 S$	Chalanata

		Arohana	Avarohana	
VII *Rishi*	37	$S\ G_1\ R_1\ G_1\ M_2\ P\ D_1\ S$	$S\ N_1\ D_1\ P\ M_2\ G_1\ R_1\ S$	Sowgandhini
	38	$S\ G_1\ R_1\ G_1\ M_2\ P\ D_1\ N_2\ S$	$S\ N_2\ D_1\ P\ M_2\ G_1\ R_1\ S$	Jaganmohanam
	39	$S\ G_1\ R_1\ G_1\ M_2\ P\ D_1\ N_3\ S$	$S\ N_3\ D_1\ P\ M_2\ G_1\ R_1\ S$	Dhalivarali
	40	$S\ G_1\ R_1\ G_1\ M_2\ P\ D_2\ P\ N_2\ S$	$S\ N_2\ D_2\ P\ M_2\ G_1\ R_1\ S$	Nabhomani
	41	$S\ G_1\ R_1\ G_1\ M_2\ P\ N_3\ D_2\ N_3\ S$	$S\ N_3\ D_2\ P\ M_2\ G_1\ R_1\ S$	Kumbhini
	42	$S\ G_1\ R_1\ G_1\ M_2\ P\ N_3\ D_3\ N_3\ S$	$S\ N_3\ P\ M_2\ G_1\ R_1\ S$	Ravikriya
VIII *Vasu*	43	$S\ R_1\ G_2\ M_2\ P\ D_1\ N1\ D_1\ P\ D_1\ S$	$S\ N_1\ D_1\ P\ M_2\ G_2\ R_1\ S$	Girvani
	44	$S\ R_1\ G_2\ M_2\ P\ D_1\ P\ N_2\ S$	$S\ N_2\ D_1\ P\ M_2\ G_2\ R_1\ S$	Bhavani
	45	$S\ R_1\ G_2\ M_2\ P\ D_1\ N_3\ S$	$S\ N_3\ D_1\ P\ M_2\ G_2\ R_1\ S$	Shivapantuvarali
	46	$S\ R_1\ M_2\ P\ D_2\ S$	$S\ N_2\ D_2\ P\ M_2\ G_2\ S$	Stavaraja
	47	$S\ R_1\ G_2\ M_2\ P\ D_2\ N_3\ S$	$S\ N_3\ D_2\ M_2\ G_2\ R_1\ S$	Sowveera
	48	$S\ R_1\ G_2\ M_2\ P\ D_3\ N_3\ S$	$S\ N_3\ P\ M_2\ G_2\ R_1\ S$	Jeevantika

		Ascending	Descending	
IX *Brahma*	49	S R$_1$ G$_3$ M$_2$ P D$_1$ S	S N$_1$ D$_1$ P M$_2$ G$_3$ R$_1$ S	Dhavalangam
	50	S R$_1$ G$_3$ M$_2$ P D$_1$ N$_2$ S	S N$_2$ D$_1$ P M$_2$ G$_3$ R$_1$ S	Namadeshi
	51	S G$_3$ R$_1$ G$_3$ M$_2$ P D$_1$ N$_3$ S	S N$_3$ D$_1$ P M$_2$ G$_3$ R$_1$ S	Kashiramakriya
	52	S R$_1$ G$_3$ M$_2$ P D$_2$ N$_2$ S	S N$_2$ D$_2$ P M$_2$ G$_3$ R$_1$ S	Ramamanohari
	53	S R$_1$ G$_3$ M$_2$ P D$_2$ P S	S N$_3$ D$_2$ P M$_2$ G$_3$ R$_1$ S	Gamakakriya
	54	S R$_1$ G$_3$ M$_2$ P D$_3$ N$_3$ S	S N$_3$ P M$_2$ G$_3$ R$_1$ S	VAmshavati
X *Dishi*	55	S R$_2$ G$_2$ M$_2$ P D$_1$ S	S N$_1$ D$_1$ P M$_2$ G$_2$ R$_2$ S	Shamala
	56	S R$_2$ G$_2$ M$_2$ P D$_1$ N$_2$ S	S N$_2$ D$_1$ P M$_2$ G$_2$ R$_2$ S	Chamara
	57	S R$_2$ G$_2$ M$_2$ P D$_1$ N$_3$ S	S N$_3$ D$_1$ P M$_2$ G$_2$ R$_2$ S	Sumadyuti
	58	S R$_2$ G$_2$ M$_2$ P D$_2$ N$_2$ S	S N$_2$ D$_2$ P M$_2$ G$_2$ R$_2$ S	Deshisimharavam
	59	S R$_2$ G$_2$ M$_2$ P D$_2$ N$_3$ S	S N$_3$ D$_2$ P M$_2$ G$_2$ R$_2$ S	Dhaamavati
	60	S R$_2$ G$_2$ M$_2$ P D$_3$ N$_3$ S	S N$_3$ P M$_2$ G$_2$ R$_2$ S	Nishada

XI *Rudra*	61	$S\ R_2\ G_3\ M_2\ P\ D_1\ S$	$S\ N_1\ D_1\ P\ M_2\ G_3\ R_2\ S$	Kuntala
	62	$S\ R_2\ G_3\ M_2\ P\ D_1\ N_2\ S$	$S\ N_2\ D_1\ P\ M_2\ G_3\ R_2\ S$	Ratipriya
	63	$S\ R_2\ G_3\ M_2\ P\ D_1\ N_3\ S$	$S\ N_3\ D_1\ P\ M_2\ G_3\ R_2\ S$	Geetapriya
	64	$S\ R_2\ G_3\ M_2\ P\ D_2\ N_2\ S$	$S\ N_2\ D_2\ P\ M_2\ G_3\ R_2\ S$	Bhushavati
	65	$S\ R_2\ G_3\ M_2\ P\ D_2\ N_3\ S$	$S\ N_3\ D_2\ P\ M_2\ G_3\ R_2\ S$	Shantakalyani
	66	$S\ R_2\ G_3\ M_2\ P\ D_3\ N_3\ S$	$S\ N_3\ P\ M_2\ G_3\ R_2\ S$	Chaturangini
XII *Aditya*	67	$S\ R_3\ G_3\ M_2\ P\ D_1\ S$	$S\ N_1\ D_1\ P\ M_2\ R_3\ S$	Santanamanjari
	68	$S\ R_3\ G_3\ M_2\ P\ D_1\ N_2\ S$	$S\ N_2\ D_1\ P\ M_2\ G_3\ S$	Joti
	69	$S\ R_3\ G_3\ M_2\ P\ D_1\ N_3\ S$	$S\ N_3\ D_1\ P\ M_2\ R_3\ G_3\ S$	Dhowtapanchamam
	70	$S\ R_3\ G_3\ M_2\ P\ D_2\ N_2\ S$	$S\ N_2\ D_2\ P\ M_2\ R_3\ G_3\ S$	Nasamani
	71	$S\ R_3\ G_3\ M_2\ P\ D_2\ N_3\ S$	$S\ N_3\ D_2\ P\ M_2\ R_3\ G_3\ S$	Kusumakara
	72	$S\ R_3\ G_3\ S\ P\ M_2\ P\ N_3\ D_3\ N_3\ S$	$S\ N_3\ D_3\ N_3\ P\ M_2\ P\ R_3\ G_3\ S$	Rasamanjari

The Modern Mela Classification

Govindacharya's **Sangraha Choodamani** is considered to be one of the last Sanskrit *grantha*s before the modern era. In addition to the theory of twenty-two *sruti*s, Govindacharya gave thirty *shuddha* and *vikruta swara*s, which can overlap. They are:

1. *Shadja*
2. *Prati Shuddha Rishabha*
3. *Shuddha Rishabha*
4. *Prati Chatusruti Rishabha*
5. *Chatusruti Rishabha*
6. *Prati Shatsruti Rishabha*
7. *Shatsruti Rishabha*
8. *Prati Shuddha Gandhara*
9. *Shuddha Gandhara*
10. *Prati Sadharana Gandhara*
11. *Sadharana Gandhara*
12. *Pratyantara Gandhara*
13. *Antara Gandhara*
14. *Prati Shuddha Madhyama*
15. *Shuddha Madhyama*
16. *Aprati Madhyama*
17. *Prati Madhyama*
18. *Panchama*
19. *Prati Shuddha Dhaivata*
20. *Shuddha Dhaivata*
21. *Prati Chatusruti Dhaivata*
22. *Chatusruti Dhaivata*

23. *Prati Shatsruti Dhaivata*
24. *Shatsruti Dhaivata*
25. *Prati Shuddha Nishada*
26. *Shuddha Nishada*
27. *Prati Kaishiki Nishada*
28. *Kaishiki Nishada*
29. *Prati Kakali Nishada*
30. *Kakali Nishada*

With regard to *Rishabha*, *Gandhara*, *Dhaivata* and *Nishada*, *prati* indicated a lower pitch, whereas with *Madhyama*, *prati* indicates a higher pitch. However, while describing *ragas*, he used only the twelve *swarasthanas*, while the other *sruti*s can be sung practically on occasion.

The present Carnatic melodic system is based on Govindacharya's *melakarta* concept, with seventy-two *melakarta* or *janaka* (parent) scales and thousands of *janya* or derived scales.

He mentions the following characteristics of *mela*s:

- The *raga* must contain one each of the seven notes (*Sa, Ri, Ga, Ma, Pa, Da, Ni*).
- All the seven notes must be in sequence.
- They must be the same in the ascending and descending.
- There should not be any other (foreign) note in the scale.

Table 12: *Melakarta Ragas*

Chakra Name					Ascending					Mela
I *Indu*	1	S	R_1	G_1	M_1	P	D_1	N_1	S	Kanakangi
	2	S	R_1	G_1	M_1	P	D_1	N_2	S	Ratnangi
	3	S	R_1	G_1	M_1	P	D_1	N_3	S	Ganamurti
	4	S	R_1	G_1	M_1	P	D_2	N_2	S	Vanaspati
	5	S	R_1	G_1	M_1	P	D_2	N_3	S	Manavati
	6	S	R_1	G_1	M_1	P	D_3	N_3	S	Tanarupi
II *Netra*	7	S	R_1	G_2	M_1	P	D_1	N_1	S	Senavati
	8	S	R_1	G_2	M_1	P	D_1	N_2	S	Hanumatodi
	9	S	R_1	G_2	M_1	P	D_1	N_3	S	Dhenuka
	10	S	R_1	G_2	M_1	P	D_2	N_2	S	Natakapriya
	11	S	R_1	G_2	M_1	P	D_2	N_3	S	Kokilapriya
	12	S	R_1	G_2	M_1	P	D_3	N_3	S	Rupavati

Group	No.									Raga
III *Agni*	13	S	R_1	G_3	M_1	P	D_1	N_1	S	Gayakapriya
	14	S	R_1	G_3	M_1	P	D_1	N_2	S	Vakulabharanam
	15	S	R_1	G_3	M_1	P	D_1	N_3	S	Mayamalavagaula
	16	S	R_1	G_3	M_1	P	D_2	N_2	S	Chakravakam
	17	S	R_1	G_3	M_1	P	D_2	N_3	S	Suryakantam
	18	S	R_1	G_3	M_1	P	D_3	N_3	S	Hatakambari
IV *Veda*	19	S	R_2	G_2	M_1	P	D_1	N_1	S	Jhankaradhvani
	20	S	R_2	G_2	M_1	P	D_1	N_2	S	Natabhairavi
	21	S	R_2	G_2	M_1	P	D_1	N_3	S	Kiravani
	22	S	R_2	G_2	M_1	P	D_2	N_2	S	Kharaharapriya
	23	S	R_2	G_2	M_1	P	D_2	N_3	S	Gourimanohari
	24	S	R_2	G_2	M_1	P	D_3	N_3	S	Varunapriya

V *Baana*	25	S	R_2	G_3	M_1	P	D_1	N_1	S	Mararanjani
	26	S	R_2	G_3	M_1	P	D_1	N_2	S	Charukesi
	27	S	R_2	G_3	M_1	P	D_1	N_3	S	Sarasangi
	28	S	R_2	G_3	M_1	P	D_2	N_2	S	Harikambhoji
	29	S	R_2	G_3	M_1	P	D_2	N_3	S	Dhirasankara-bharanam
	30	S	R_2	G_3	M_1	P	D_3	N_3	S	Naganandini
VI *Ritu*	31	S	R_3	G_3	M_1	P	D_1	N_1	S	Yagapriya
	32	S	R_3	G_3	M_1	P	D_1	N_2	S	Ragavardhani
	33	S	R_3	G_3	M_1	P	D_1	N_3	S	Gangeyabhushani
	34	S	R_3	G_3	M_1	P	D_2	N_2	S	Vagadhisvari
	35	S	R_3	G_3	M_1	P	D_2	N_3	S	Sulini
	36	S	R_3	G_3	M_1	P	D_3	N_3	S	Chalanata

VII *Rishi*	37	S	R_1	G_1	M_2	P	D_1	N_1	S	Salagam
	38	S	R_1	G_1	M_2	P	D_1	N_2	S	Jalarnavam
	39	S	R_1	G_1	M_2	P	D_1	N_3	S	Jhalavarali
	40	S	R_1	G_1	M_2	P	D_2	N_2	S	Navanitam
	41	S	R_1	G_1	M_2	P	D_2	N_3	S	Pavani
	42	S	R_1	G_1	M_2	P	D_3	N_3	S	Raghupriya
VIII *Vasu*	43	S	R_1	G_2	M_2	P	D_1	N_1	S	Gavambhodi
	44	S	R_1	G_2	M_2	P	D_1	N_2	S	Bhavapriya
	45	S	R_1	G_2	M_2	P	D_1	N_3	S	Shubhapantuvarali
	46	S	R_1	G_2	M_2	P	D_2	N_2	S	Shadvidhamargini
	47	S	R_1	G_2	M_2	P	D_2	N_3	S	Suvarnangi
	48	S	R_1	G_2	M_2	P	D_3	N_3	S	Divyamani

IX *Brahma*	49	S	R_1	G_3	M_2	P	D_1	N_1	S	Dhavalambari
	50	S	R_1	G_3	M_2	P	D_1	N_2	S	Namanarayani
	51	S	R_1	G_3	M_2	P	D_1	N_3	S	Kamavardhini
	52	S	R_1	G_3	M_2	P	D_2	N_2	S	Ramapriya
	53	S	R_1	G_3	M_2	P	D_2	N_3	S	Gamanashrama
	54	S	R_1	G_3	M_2	P	D_3	N_3	S	Vishvambari
X *Dishi*	55	S	R_2	G_2	M_2	P	D_1	N_1	S	Shyamalangi
	56	S	R_2	G_2	M_2	P	D_1	N_2	S	Shanmukhapriya
	57	S	R_2	G_2	M_2	P	D_1	N_3	S	Simhendramadhyamam
	58	S	R_2	G_2	M_2	P	D_2	N_2	S	Hemavati
	59	S	R_2	G_2	M_2	P	D_2	N_3	S	Dharmavati
	60	S	R_2	G_2	M_2	P	D_3	N_3	S	Nitimati

XI *Rudra*	61	S	R_2	G_3	M_2	P	D_1	N_1	S	Kantamani
	62	S	R_2	G_3	M_2	P	D_1	N_2	S	Rishabhapriya
	63	S	R_2	G_3	M_2	P	D_1	N_3	S	Latangi
	64	S	R_2	G_3	M_2	P	D_2	N_2	S	Vachaspati
	65	S	R_2	G_3	M_2	P	D_2	N_3	S	Mechakalyani
	66	S	R_2	G_3	M_2	P	D_3	N_3	S	Chitrambari
XII *Aditya*	67	S	R_3	G_3	M_2	P	D_1	N_1	S	Sucharitra
	68	S	R_3	G_3	M_2	P	D_1	N_2	S	Jyotisvarupini
	69	S	R_3	G_3	M_2	P	D_1	N_3	S	Dhatuvardhani
	70	S	R_3	G_3	M_2	P	D_2	N_2	S	Nasikabhushani
	71	S	R_3	G_3	M_2	P	D_2	N_3	S	Kosalam
	72	S	R_3	G_3	M_2	P	D_3	N_3	S	Rasikapriya

Dr L. Subramaniam conducting his composition 'Global Symphony' featuring Kavita Krishnamurti and soloist Arve Tellefsen with Oslo Camerata at the Lakshminarayana Global Music Festival, New Delhi.

Dr L. Subramaniam conducting his composition 'Spring Rhapsody' performed by the London Symphony Orchestra at the Barbican Centre, London.

World premiere of the 'Bharat Symphony' concert commissioned by the Chicago World Music Festival at the Jay Pritzker Pavilion, Millenium Park - Chicago. Seen in the picture Kavita Krishnamurti, Bindu and Mahati Subramaniam.

Kavita Krishnamurti performing the 'Bharat Symphony' written by Dr L. Subramaniam for the 70th year of India's Independence celebrations with the London Symphony Orchestra and the London Voices at the Barbican Centre.

Kavita Krishnamurti performing the 'Freedom Symphony' composed
by Dr L. Subramaniam with the Royal Oman Symphony at the
Royal Opera House, Muscat.

Dr L. Subramaniam performing his composition 'Turbulence Concerto'
with Ambi Subramaniam and the Leipzig Philharmonic Orchestra
in Hampi, India.

Dr L. Subramaniam conducting one of his compositions for the
Halle Symphony Orchestra from East Germany.

Dr L. Subramaniam with Lord Yehudi Menuhin performing his
raga-based composition 'Journey' at the United Nations, New York.

Dr L. Subramaniam with Stephane Grapelli recording
his composition 'Conversations'.

Dr L. Subramaniam with Viji Subramaniam after the premiere
of his work 'Fantasy on Vedic Chants' with the New York
Philharmonic conducted by Maestro Zubin Mehta at the
Avery Fisher Hall, Lincoln Centre, New York.

Dr L. Subramaniam performing his composition 'Shanti Priya' with
the Houston Symphony at the Hobby Center, Houston.

Kavita Krishnamurti performing the 'Mahatma Symphony' with the OSCyL
at the National Theatre, Madrid.

Performing the 'Paris Concerto' with the Orchestre de chambre de Paris conducted by Maestro Josep Vicent at the Philharmonie de Paris.

Dr L. Subramaniam's raga-based composition 'Don't leave me' re-recorded with A.R. Rahman, Bindu Subramaniam, Mahati Subramaniam, Khatija Rahman, Raheema Rahman and A.R. Ameen.

Dr L. Subramaniam performing 'Fantasy on Vedic Chants' in East Berlin with the Rais Symphony and Berlin Opera. The concert was broadcast on the radio simultaneously in close to 100 countries.

Derived *Ragas*

From these *mela* or *janaka* (parent) *ragas*, thousands of *janya ragas* can be derived. There are three main ways of deriving *ragas*:

1. By omitting one or more notes (*varja ragas*)
2. By rearraging the order of the notes (*vakra ragas*)
3. By adding a foreign note (*bhashanga ragas*)

These additions or omissions can be only in the ascending, only in the descending, or in both. *Ragas* can also use a combination of *varja*, *vakra* and *bhashanga* types.

Ragas with five notes are known as *audava*, those with six notes are called *shadava* and *ragas* with seven notes are known as *sampoorna*.

Ragas are based on scales, but scales played are not considered *ragas*, because a *raga* includes ornamentation and emphasis on certain primary notes (the *vadi* being the most significant note and the *samvadi* being the second most important). The *vadi* is in the first tetrachord (*purva anga*) and the *samvadi* can be the fourth or the fifth note. The *samvadi* is said to emphasise the importance of the *vadi*. The remaining notes are known as *anuvadi* or residual notes. The notes which are dissonant, and do not belong to the *raga*, are known as *vivadi swaras*.

It is useful to remember that although *ragas* are based on scales, they do not have key signatures. This is because key signatures presuppose a fixed key, but a *raga* can be sung in any key, and the relative intervals are more important than the key of the tonic. In this way, *ragas* are closer to modes than keys, because modes also are dependent on intervals and not keys.

Another characteristic feature of Carnatic music is its use of microtones, which are often less than a quartertone. Instead of dividing an octave into twelve semitones like in the West, an octave is divided into twenty-two *sruti*s (tones). Based on this system, the tonic and the dominant are always fixed and can be only one tone each. The rest five of the seven notes (the supertonic or *Ri*, median or *Ga*, subdominant or *Ma*, submediant or *Da* and the leading note or *Ni*) can each be of four types. Thus, they are twenty-two *sruti*s.

Derivation of *Sampoorna* Scales from the *Melakartas*

P. Sambamoorthy presented the idea of 5,184 *raga*s, which has been expanded upon as follows:

Taking the ascending of the first *melakarta* (Kanakangi) and using each of the seventy-two as descending, from Kanakangi to Rasikapriya, we can get seventy-two *sampoorna* scales. Following a similar pattern, we can use the second *melakarta* (Ratnangi) for ascending, and each of the seventy-two for descending, starting from Kanakangi, once again to Rasikapriya.

By using all the seventy-two, one by one in ascending, and for each, the seventy-two in descending, we will have 72 x 72 = 5,184 sampoorna scales.

It will be easy to identify the scales if we call it Kanakangi if it is Kanakangi in both ascending and descending, and Kanakangi/Ratnangi if it is Kanakangi in ascending and Ratnangi in descending. This way, it will continue to follow the existing nomenclature.

Derivation of 62,208 Sampoorna Scales

Western classical music deals with the concept of twelve notes (see Table 13).

Table 13: Western Classical Music Notes

Note	Enharmonic
C	
C#	Db
D	
D#	Eb
E	
F	
F#	Gb
G	
G#	Ab
A	
A#	Bb
B	

These notes are also called tonic, supertonic, mediant, subdominant, dominant, submediant and subtonic or leading note.

In Western classical music, pitch tonalities are fixed according to frequencies. For example, if the frequency of A (in the fourth octave on a piano) is fixed at 440 Hz, it will always be fixed at that. Orchestras in different parts of the world can tune at 438Hz or 442Hz, but there is no great fluctuation, as in Indian music, where *Sa* can literally be at any frequency. (In Indian music, pitch is relative to the tonic or *Sa*. Therefore, R_1 would be considered R_1, whether *Sa* is C or D or any other note.)

This system in Western classical music is possibly because, when a number of instruments have to be played together in an ensemble or orchestral format, where there can even be a hundred musicians playing simultaneously, it is important that the tuning pitches be fixed.

Table 14: Frequencies for equal tempered scale, A4 = 440 Hz

Note	Frequency (Hz)	Wavelength (cm)
C_0	16.35	2109.89
$C^\#_0/D^b_0$	17.32	1991.47
D_0	18.35	1879.69
$D^\#_0/E^b_0$	19.45	1774.20
E_0	20.60	1674.62
F_0	21.83	1580.63
$F^\#_0/G^b_0$	23.12	1491.91
G_0	24.50	1408.18
$G^\#_0/A^b_0$	25.96	1329.14

A_0	27.50	1254.55
$A^\#_0/B^b_0$	29.14	1184.13
B_0	30.87	1117.67
C_1	32.70	1054.94
$C^\#_1/D^b_1$	34.65	995.73
D_1	36.71	939.85
$D^\#_1/E^b_1$	38.89	887.10
E_1	41.20	837.31
F_1	43.65	790.31
$F^\#_1/G^b_1$	46.25	745.96
G_1	49.00	704.09
$G^\#_1/A^b_1$	51.91	664.57
A_1	55.00	627.27
$A^\#_1/B^b_1$	58.27	592.07
B_1	61.74	558.84
C_2	65.41	527.47
$C^\#_2/D^b_2$	69.30	497.87
D_2	73.42	469.92
$D^\#_2/E^b_2$	77.78	443.55
E_2	82.41	418.65
F_2	87.31	395.16
$F^\#_2/G^b_2$	92.50	372.98
G_2	98.00	352.04
$G^\#_2/A^b_2$	103.83	332.29

A_2	110.00	313.64
$A^{\#}_2/B^{b}_2$	116.54	296.03
B_2	123.47	279.42
C_3	130.81	263.74
$C^{\#}_3/D^{b}_3$	138.59	248.93
D_3	146.83	234.96
$D^{\#}_3/E^{b}_3$	155.56	221.77
E_3	164.81	209.33
F_3	174.61	197.58
$F^{\#}_3/G^{b}_3$	185.00	186.49
G_3	196.00	176.02
$G^{\#}_3/A^{b}_3$	207.65	166.14
A_3	220.00	156.82
$A^{\#}_3/B^{b}_3$	233.08	148.02
B_3	246.94	139.71
C_4	261.63	131.87
$C^{\#}_4/D^{b}_4$	277.18	124.47
D_4	293.66	117.48
$D^{\#}_4/E^{b}_4$	311.13	110.89
E_4	329.63	104.66
F_4	349.23	98.79
$F^{\#}_4/G^{b}_4$	369.99	93.24
G_4	392.00	88.01
$G^{\#}_4/A^{b}_4$	415.30	83.07

A_4	440.00	78.41
$A^{\#}_4/B^b_4$	466.16	74.01
B_4	493.88	69.85
C_5	523.25	65.93
$C^{\#}_5/D^b_5$	554.37	62.23
D_5	587.33	58.74
$D^{\#}_5/E^b_5$	622.25	55.44
E_5	659.25	52.33
F_5	698.46	49.39
$F^{\#}_5/G^b_5$	739.99	46.62
G_5	783.99	44.01
$G^{\#}_5/A^b_5$	830.61	41.54
A_5	880.00	39.20
$A^{\#}_5/B^b_5$	932.33	37.00
B_5	987.77	34.93
C_6	1046.50	32.97
$C^{\#}_6/D^b_6$	1108.73	31.12
D_6	1174.66	29.37
$D^{\#}_6/E^b_6$	1244.51	27.72
E_6	1318.51	26.17
F_6	1396.91	24.70
$F^{\#}_6/G^b_6$	1479.98	23.31
G_6	1567.98	22.00
$G^{\#}_6/A^b_6$	1661.22	20.77

A_6	1760.00	19.60
$A^{\#}_6/B^b_6$	1864.66	18.50
B_6	1975.53	17.46
C_7	2093.00	16.48
$C^{\#}_7/D^b_7$	2217.46	15.56
D_7	2349.32	14.69
$D^{\#}_7/E^b_7$	2489.02	13.86
E_7	2637.02	13.08
F_7	2793.83	12.35
$F^{\#}_7/G^b_7$	2959.96	11.66
G_7	3135.96	11.00
$G^{\#}_7/A^b_7$	3322.44	10.38
A_7	3520.00	9.80
$A^{\#}_7/B^b_7$	3729.31	9.25
B_7	3951.07	8.73
C_8	4186.01	8.24
$C^{\#}_8/D^b_8$	4434.92	7.78
D_8	4698.63	7.34
$D^{\#}_8/E^b_8$	4978.03	6.93
E_8	5274.04	6.54
F_8	5587.65	6.17
$F^{\#}_8/G^b_8$	5919.91	5.83
G_8	6271.93	5.50
$G^{\#}_8/A^b_8$	6644.88	5.19

A_8	7040.00	4.90
$A^\#_8/B^b_8$	7458.62	4.63
B_8	7902.13	4.37

According to the Western scale concept, there are a few scales that have seven notes:

1. Major Scale: Where the interval between the notes is tone, tone, semitone, tone, tone, tone, semitone; for example, a C major scale, which has the notes C, D, E, F, G, A, B. This scale corresponds to the scale of *Raga* Shankarabharana in Carnatic music.

2. Natural Minor Scale: Where the interval between the notes is tone, semitone, tone, tone, semitone, tone, tone; for example, an A minor scale, which has the notes A, B, C, D, E, F, G. Other variations of the minor scale are harmonic (where the seventh note is sharpened on the ascending and the descending) and melodic minor scales (where the sixth and seventh notes are sharpened on the ascending alone).

Although the intervals or patterns between tones and semitones stay the same, for all major scales, there are twelve major scales—one for each note, and an A major scale is different from a C major scale. This is because frequencies vary for each scale.

Adapting this logic, each of the 5,184 scales can be produced in each of the twelve notes of the Western scale, creating a total of 62,208 unique scales.

The Difference between Scales and *Ragas*

The 5,184 scales can be made into *ragas* by following the rules which create a *raga*, like by creating a vadi, samvadi, and some typical phrases with ornamentation.

In a *raga*, the different types of notes are:

1. *Vadi*: The *swara* which plays the most important part
2. *Samvadi*: Any two *swara*s which are at an interval of nine or thirteen *sruti*s from each other and are mutually consonant
3. *Vivadi*: If the notes are at an interval of two *sruti*s and the *swara* sounds discordant to another
4. *Anuvadi*: The assonant notes remaining after *vadi*, *samvadi* and *vivadi*

Vadi and *samvadi* are the primary notes, which are emphasised during *raga* development. Usually from the *vadi*, the fourth or fifth note becomes the *samvadi*.

These notes can be emphasised in different ways:

1. By repeating the note more frequently than other notes
2. By holding the notes for a longer duration than other notes
3. By keeping the note as tonal centre, developing around it and coming back to that note as a resting note

In *raga*s, certain notes are ornamented with slides, known as *gamaka*s. In certain cases, multiple slides are used for the same note. It is also common to slide towards a note, from a note below or from a note above, and it is even possible to slide more than one note interval, and in different directions to reach a note, in order to bring in the essence of the *raga*.

These will give a particular colour and mood to the *raga*. There should be a *graha swara, anuswara* and *nyasa swara*.

In any *raga*, in order to create a composition, it is necessary to have some scope for development. It is also important to create a certain mood or essence, or feeling for someone who is listening to the *raga*.

If we create 5,184 *ragas* by following the above rules, they cannot be expanded into 62,208 by multiplying into the twelve semitones. This is so because whichever semitone is used, the relative interval will stay the same. For example, Shankarabharanam is the same *raga* whether it is in C, C# or D.

Making a Scale into a *Raga* and Creating a Composition

An example of this is the new *raga* of Vacharamapriya, using the ascending of *raga* Vachaspati and the descending of *raga* Ramapriya. The name of the *raga* still follows the Katapayadi system, making it possible to derive the number of the scale.

The vadi is *Antara Gandhara* or G_3, as it typically is whenever it is present in a *raga*. It is the *amsha swara*.

The *samvadi* is D_2, and typically G_3 and N_2 could be ornamented with *gamaka*s. The R_1 is a *vivadi swara*.

The composition is as follows:

Aarohana: S R_2 G_3 M_2 P D_2 N_2 **S** (Vachaspati)

Avarohana: **S** N_2 D_2 P M_2 G_3 R_1 S (Ramapriya)

,GMP MGG, ,R$_2$MP MGG, ||
,MPD PMM, ,R$_2$MP DMM, ||
,MPD PGR$_1$, ,MGR$_1$ GR$_1$ S,||

4

Practical Application of *Raga* Harmony

In harmony, we use multiple notes; ideally, a minimum of three notes to create a vertical motion with polyphony. The notes supplement each other to create a pleasant, interesting progression for the development of the melody along with the supplementary notes, which create the harmony.

Expansion of the *Raga* System

The expansion of 72 x 72, resulting in 5,184 scales as laid out by Professor Sambamoorthy, can be further expanded with the Western concept of taking each semitone as the tonic, resulting in 62,208 scales, each of which can be treated with *Raga* Harmony.

Raga Harmony is a concept where we create multiple tonalities using only the *swaras* or notes of the *raga*. Since some of the *ragas* have unusual intervals, the polytonal possibilities can create newer tonalities, which are not commonly used in the traditional concept of Western harmony.

It expands the existing possibilities of harmony in accordance with the Western classical system, while at the same time introducing the concept of harmony legitimately into the concept of Indian classical music. The importance of *Raga* Harmony is that it adheres to the rules of both Indian and Western classical music, and has the potential to enhance both.

After theoretically examining the concept of *Raga* Harmony, it is useful to examine its practical applications. Over the last three decades, I have experimented and developed the concept of *Raga* Harmony and I have implemented it in a number of compositions written for orchestras, where the parts that comprise the harmony are given to many different instruments within the orchestral structure.

Before delving into this, it would be helpful to take a traditional Carnatic *raga* and identify harmonic possibilities available within the *raga*.

Raga Charukesi

Raga Charukesi takes the twenty-sixth slot in the list of seventy-two *melas*. According to *Asampoorna mela paddhati*, this *raga* is called Tarangini and takes the *swaras Shadja, Chatusruti Rishabha, Antara Gandhara, Shuddha Madhyama, Panchama, Shuddha Dhaivata* and *Kaishiki Nishada*.

The first mention of this *raga* is found in the Appendix of *Chaturdandi Prakashika* called *Raga-lakshana* written by Muddu Venkatamakhi, the grandson of Venkatamakhi, dating back to the early eighteenth century. But in this, he gives the *raga-lakshana* as the absence of *Rishabha* and *Gandhara* in *aarohana* (ascent) and in *avarohana* (descent) all the seven notes but in zig-zag order. But together this *mela* takes all the seven notes. The *shadja swara* is the *graha swara*.

Subbarama Dikshitar in **Sangeeta Sampradaya Pradarshini** (1904 CE) mentioned that *Madhyama* and *Nishada* are absent in the *aarohana* (ascent). Though *Nishada* is mentioned in the *aarohana* it appears in the phrase N D P, which obviously is a descent.

Aarohana—S R_2 G_3 P D_1 N_2 D_1 P D_1 **S**

Avarohana—**S** D_1 P G_3 R_2 S R_2 G_3 M_1 G_3 R_2 S

According to this text, *Shadja* is *graha swara*; *Rishabha* is *amsha*, *graha* and *nyasa swara*.

But in *Sampoorna Mela Paddhati*, which was formulated by Govindacharya, the twenty-sixth mela is called Charukesi. Tarangini, which existed till then as the twenty-sixth mela became a *janya* or derived *raga* of Charukesi.

Charukesi's scale is:

S R_2 G_3 M_1 P D_1 N_2 **S**

S N_2 D_1 P M_1 G_3 R_2 S.

Harmonic Structure Available

Taking *Sa* as E, the scale of Charukesi in Western notation is:

E F# G# A B C D

The harmonic structures available are as follows:

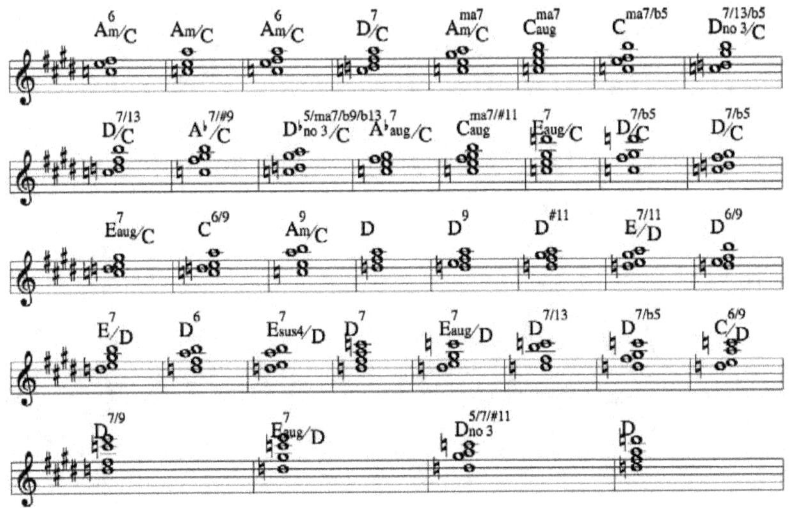

Application in *Shanti Priya*

In the composition *Shanti Priya*, which I wrote in 1987, the *Raga* Harmony of Charukesi was utilised as follows:

Shanti Priya

Raga: Charukesi; Tala: Eka

Aro: S R_2 G_3 M_1 P D_1 N_2 **S**

Ava: **S** N_2 D_1 P M_1 G_3 R_2 S
   ,, P, D**M** ,**G** || **G**, ,, ,, ,,||
   ,, **GM MP GM**,,|| **R**, ,, ,, ,,||
   ,, **RG GM RG**,,|| **RS**,, ,, ,, ,, ||
   ,, **S**, **RR** ,**G**|| N, ,, ,, SNDP||
   D, ,, ,, ,,||

Andante guisto
Fl. 1, 2
Cl. 1, 2
Bsn. 1, 2
Hn. 3, 4
Hp.
Andante guisto
Cb.

Adagio Rubato
Hp.
Adagio Rubato
S Vn.
Vln. I
Vln. II
Vla.
Vc.
Cb.

Bsn. 1, 2
freely (quasi improvisation)
S Vn.
Vln. I
Vln. II
Vla.
Vc.
Cb.

It is important to note that in this composition, and indeed in all orchestral compositions that I have created using the concept of *Raga* Harmony, the melodic lines are played by a number of different instruments: the strings section (including violins, violas, cellos and double bass), the woodwinds section (including flute, oboe, clarinet and bassoon), the brass section (including trumpet, trombone and tuba) and the harp. Each individual instrumentalist is contributing towards the composition without having to understand the *raga* concept, as the line is notated in Western notation.

Another example of *Raga* Harmony can be examined as below, with *Raga* Shanmukhapriya:

Shanmukhapriya

Raga Shanmukhapriya is the fifty-sixth *melakarta*. This was called Chamara in the *Asampoorna mela paddhati* and later called Shanmukhapriya in the *Sampoorna mela paddhati*. It takes the *swaras Shadja, Chatusruti Rishabha, Sadharana Gandhara, Prati Madhyama, Panchama, Shuddha Dhaivata* and *Kaishiki Nishada*. In both the systems, the ascent and descent are the same, with the *swaras* placed in an order of succession:

S R G M P D N **S—S** N D P M G R S

Panchama is the *Amsha swara*; *Rishabha, Madhyama* and *Dhaivata* are *nyasa swaras* in this *raga*. Shanmukhapriya is a melodious *raga* with exquisite beauty and a blissful pleasing quality.

This *mela* gives new *sampoorna* scales when it undergoes modal shift of the tonic (*graha bheda*).

When *Gandhara* is taken as the tonic note it gives rise to Shoolini, *Panchama* as the tonic note gives rise to Dhenuka and *Dhaivata* as the tonic note gives rise to Chitrambari.

In Western notation, keeping *Sa* as D, the notation of Shanmukhapriya is:

D E F G# A Bb C D

Harmonic Structure Available

Application in *Paris Concerto*

This particular concerto of mine starts with *Sa* and uses the scale and *Raga* Harmony. The second phrase takes *Ni* as *Sa*, using the *moorchana* concept and *Raga* Harmony. The third phrase takes *Da* as *Sa*, the fourth one *Pa*. This concept of *moorchana*, or deriving scales from the original scale by going down one note each time from the tonic, has been in existence since the time of the *Natyashastra*.

Paris Concerto

Raga: Shanmukhapriya; Tala: Eka

Aro: S R_2 G_2 M_2 P D_1 N_2 **S**
Ava: **S** N_2 D_1 P M_2 G_2 R_2 S

„SG PMDP NDPM GRS,
„nG MGDM NDMG RSn,
„dS GSMG DMGR Snd,
„pn RSGR MGRS ndp,
„SG PMDP **S**NDP MGRS
„„„**S ,R,G S,,, ,,,,**
„„„**N ,S,R N,,, ,,,,**
N,,, **S,,, R,,, ,,,,**
D,,, P,,, S,,, ,,,,

Paris Concerto
Movt I
L. Subramaniam
♩=86
Flute
Alto Flute
Oboe
English Horn
Clarinet in B♭
Percussion
Timpani
Tambourine
♩=86
Violin I
Violin II
Viola
Violoncello
Double Bass
Fl.
A. Fl.
Bsn.
Pno.
Vln. I
Vln. II
Vla.
Vc.
Db.

5

The New Concept of
Thirty-Six Scales: An Analysis

So far, we have seen the development of the *raga* system, up to the seventy-two *melakarta* system, propounded by Venkatamakhi and the system propounded by Govindacharya. We have further seen Professor Sambamoorthy's expansion of 5,184 *melakarta* ragas, and I have expanded them further into 62,208 scales by applying the system of twelve tones. With the options of 62,208 *sampoorna melas*, there is definitely an almost infinite scope of both derived scales and harmonic possibilities, but the study may prove daunting.

I would like to postulate a simple system of thirty-six scales, which can be made into *ragas*. Within this new system, all other scales in the *melakarta* system and all derived scales would find a place, and this system would also give rise to innumerable harmonic possibilities. This system of thirty-six scales will be enough for any student or musician to study in order to explore and experiment with *Raga* Harmony.

This is similar to the *sampoorna* seventy-two *melakarta* system of Govindacharya in terms of progression of notes, but each *raga* has both M_1 and M_2, which are given equal weightage. This is not unlike the ancient *madhyama* concept, which allowed for the use of eight notes.

Further, this gives scope for categorising some *ragas* and scales, which cannot be correctly categorised under the *sampoorna mela paddhati* of Govindacharya. These include the North Indian *ragas* like Basant Bahaar (S M_1 P G_2 M_1 N_2 D_2 N_3 Ṡ–Ṡ N_3 D_1 P M_2 G_3 R_1 S), Behag, Lalit, Gaud Sarang, Hameer and Shyam Kalyan which have both the *madhyamas* given equal prominence in the scale. It will also cover the Western blues scale, and Locrian mode, which have both the perfect and augmented fourths.

These thirty-six scales will still have the possibility to give rise to the existing seventy-two *melakartas* by the omission of one of the *madhyamas*. Similarly, all the existing derived scales can be obtained from these thirty-six scales.

The thirty-six scales are shown on the opposite page.

1. S R1 G1 M1 M2 P D1 N1 Ṡ Ṡ N1 D1 P M2 M1 G1 R1 S

2. S R1 G1 M1 M2 P D1 N2 Ṡ Ṡ N2 D1 P M2 M1 G1 R1 S

3. S R1 G1 M1 M2 P D1 N3 Ṡ Ṡ N3 D1 P M2 M1 G1 R1 S

4. S R1 G1 M1 M2 P D2 N2 Ṡ Ṡ N2 D2 P M2 M1 G1 R1 S

5. S R1 G1 M1 M2 P D2 N3 Ṡ Ṡ N3 D2 P M2 M1 G1 R1 S

6. S R1 G1 M1 M2 P D3 N3 Ṡ Ṡ N3 D3 P M2 M1 G1 R1 S

7. S R1 G2 M1 M2 P D1 N1 Ṡ Ṡ N1 D1 P M2 M1 G2 R1 S

8. S R1 G2 M1 M2 P D1 N2 Ṡ Ṡ N2 D1 P M2 M1 G2 R1 S

9. S R1 G2 M1 M2 P D1 N3 Ṡ Ṡ N3 D1 P M2 M1 G2 R1 S

10. S R1 G2 M1 M2 P D2 N2 Ṡ Ṡ N2 D2 P M2 M1 G2 R1 S

11. S R1 G2 M1 M2 P D2 N3 Ṡ   Ṡ N3 D2 P M2 M1 G2 R1 S

12. S R1 G2 M1 M2 P D3 N3 Ṡ   Ṡ N3 D3 P M2 M1 G2 R1 S

13. S R1 G3 M1 M2 P D1 N1 Ṡ   Ṡ N1 D1 P M2 M1 G3 R1 S

14. S R1 G3 M1 M2 P D1 N2 Ṡ   Ṡ N2 D1 P M2 M1 G3 R1 S

15. S R1 G3 M1 M2 P D1 N3 Ṡ   Ṡ N3 D1 P M2 M1 G3 R1 S

16. S R1 G3 M1 M2 P D2 N2 Ṡ Ṡ N2 D2 P M2 M1 G3 R1 S

17. S R1 G3 M1 M2 P D2 N3 Ṡ Ṡ N3 D2 P M2 M1 G3 R1 S

18. S R1 G3 M1 M2 P D3 N3 Ṡ Ṡ N3 D3 P M2 M1 G3 R1 S

19. S R2 G2 M1 M2 P D1 N1 Ṡ Ṡ N1 D1 P M2 M1 G2 R2 S

20. S R2 G2 M1 M2 P D1 N2 Ṡ Ṡ N2 D1 P M2 M1 G2 R2 S

21. S R2 G2 M1 M2 P D1 N3 Ṡ Ṡ N3 D1 P M2 M1 G2 R2 S

22. S R2 G2 M1 M2 P D2 N2 Ṡ Ṡ N2 D2 P M2 M1 G2 R2 S

23. S R2 G2 M1 M2 P D2 N3 Ṡ Ṡ N3 D2 P M2 M1 G2 R2 S

24. S R2 G2 M1 M2 P D3 N3 Ṡ Ṡ N3 D3 P M2 M1 G2 R2 S

25. S R2 G3 M1 M2 P D1 N1 Ṡ Ṡ N1 D1 P M2 M1 G3 R2 S

26. S R2 G3 M1 M2 P D1 N2 Ṡ Ṡ N2 D1 P M2 M1 G3 R2 S

27. S R2 G3 M1 M2 P D1 N3 Ṡ Ṡ N3 D1 P M2 M1 G3 R2 S

28. S R2 G3 M1 M2 P D2 N2 Ṡ Ṡ N2 D2 P M2 M1 G3 R2 S

29. S R2 G3 M1 M2 P D2 N3 Ṡ Ṡ N3 D2 P M2 M1 G3 R2 S

30. S R2 G3 M1 M2 P D3 N3 Ṡ Ṡ N3 D3 P M2 M1 G3 R2 S

30

31. S R3 G3 M1 M2 P D1 N1 Ṡ Ṡ N1 D1 P M2 M1 G3 R3 S

[6] **31**

32. S R3 G3 M1 M2 P D1 N2 Ṡ Ṡ N2 D1 P M2 M1 G3 R3 S

32

33. S R3 G3 M1 M2 P D1 N3 Ṡ Ṡ N3 D1 P M2 M1 G3 R3 S

33

34. S R3 G3 M1 M2 P D2 N2 Ṡ Ṡ N2 D2 P M2 M1 G3 R3 S

34

35. S R3 G3 M1 M2 P D2 N3 Ṡ Ṡ N3 D2 P M2 M1 G3 R3 S

36. S R3 G3 M1 M2 P D3 N3 Ṡ Ṡ N3 D3 P M2 M1 G3 R3 S

By cross-connecting the first and second halves of these thirty-six scales, that is, by having the first of the thirty-six in ascending, and each of the thirty-six in descending, and so on with the second and third and others, we can come to a system of 1,296 scales, which are outlined below. These 1,296 scales can also be further multiplied by the twelve tones, to have a new complete system of 15,552 scales.

Of these thirty-six groups of thirty-six scales, the first eighteen groups have the ascending unchanged, and only the descending changing. The nineteenth to thirty-sixth groups have the ascending changing while the descending remains unchanged. (See Appendix for the complete list of 1,296 scales in Indian and Western notation.)

Creation of a Composition Using One of the Thirty-six Scales

I have chosen one of the new thirty-six scales to create a composition with both melody and harmony, to demonstrate the possibilities available when using this new system:

Scale #18 of 36
Aro: S R_1 G_3 M_1 M_2 P D_3 N_3 S
Ava: S N_3 D_3 P M_2 M_1 G_3 R_1 S

„S G,G M_1,M_1 M_2,M_2 P,D S,, ,,, ,,,
„S NDP M_2,, M_1,, G,S N,, ,,, ,,,

It is possible to create compositions using this style and method without having a deep knowledge of the *raga* system, but instead treating these scales as regular scales and utilising the new harmonic possibilities.

Thus, it can be seen that the new system of thirty-six is rooted in the traditional system, merely taking it one step further. It also provides a simple foundation for any non-Carnatic musician to understand and follow, thereby allowing for the widespread applicability of *Raga* Harmony.

Conclusion

Music develops only through innovation, and often that innovation comes through inspiration from different traditions. In centuries past, innovation took place at a much slower pace, perhaps because the time taken for a new trend to reach the ears of an open-minded composer was much longer. In modern times, innovation in music seems to be a constant and necessary phenomenon.

Western classical music too has been dynamic for centuries, adapting and absorbing different influences and elements. There have been many earlier attempts at adding flavour to Western classical music, and music of the East has played a role in a number of instances. Every 150 years, there have been different trends in styles of musical composition from the Baroque to the Classical to the Romantic and so on. It is possible that the introduction of the new thirty-six scale pattern, based on the Carnatic *raga* tradition, can create new tonalities, and indeed a new direction of composition. There is no necessity for a composer to fully understand the *raga* system before undertaking compositions using this methodology because of the way the system has been laid out—clearly and systematically. The complexity of the *raga* system should not be a cause for apprehension for a composer.

In parallel, South Indian Classical music has developed methodically over a few thousand years and today, it is perhaps the most systematic and complete melodic and rhythmic system of music. The Western concept of harmony does not exist in Carnatic music, although arguments have been made that the *tambura* or the drone forms a sort of a pedal tone or implied harmony. Even though the concept of harmony does not exist in Carnatic music, the melodic structure of the *raga* system provides a wide variety of harmonic possibilities for any composer. Upon expanding the existing *melakarta* system further, it is possible to create an almost unlimited number of harmonies, which can be applied to any composition (orchestral or otherwise). This can infuse what are often perceived as regular or common harmonic progressions with a great deal of variety and freshness, thus further developing the realm of orchestral composition.

Expansion of the Concept of *Raga*

Raga is one of the main terms used to refer to the melodic concept, both in the South Indian (Carnatic) and North Indian (Hindustani) classical traditions.

During the eighteenth century, one of the greatest musicologists, Venkatamakhi, devised the *Melakarta* system, which recognised seventy-two parent scales from which one could develop thousands of scales, called derived scales. This concept created a logical method for deriving scales (creating *janya ragas*). Because of this, innumerable *ragas* are possible.

In Carnatic music, hundreds of compositions in many different *raga*s have been created by many of the great composers like Purandara Dasa, Tyagaraja, Dikshithar, Shyama Shastri and many more since then. This has resulted in hundreds of *raga*s being performed by different artists at any given time. More than a million scales can be derived by expanding the concept of the seventy-two parent scales.

For this reason, the South Indian *raga* system can be used to create full orchestral, symphonic works, supplementing Western harmonic structure with combinations of notes of *raga*s, to create a pleasing, vertical movement (chordal progression). This has been very common in Western symphonic composition.

Using this system, a composer of non-Indian tradition trying to compose a symphonic composition will have a great number of options available to them. This includes traditionally used chords, but also many more options, which are uncommon but pleasing to the ear. This could prove a boon to innovative composers.

Furthermore, whenever we talk about *raga*, there are certain factors which contribute to the colour, flavour, mood and emotion. These include the *vadi* (primary note in the first four notes of the *aarohana* or the ascending SRGM) and *samvadi* (second important note in the last four notes of the *aarohana* PDNS). Normally, the *samvadi* could be the fourth or fifth note from the *vadi*, so that gives scope to develop the *raga* in a balanced way. Also, in addition to the tonic (Sa), if a *raga* has the fifth (Pa), that is also commonly used as tonal centre for developing the *raga*. The secondary notes of the *raga* (*anuvadi swara*s), which are less important than the primary notes, are still essential for the development of the *raga*.

From the earlier chapters, we know it is easy to obtain thousands of *sampoorna* scales (72 x 72 = 5,184). These can be further expanded to over 62,208 scales when we consider the Western music approach with twelve semitones in an octave. We can get all these scales plus few others, which are not covered under this, with this new concept of thirty-six scales, with eight notes in an octave. One of the basic concepts of these thirty-six scales is that, in addition to the tonic (*Sa*) and the dominant (*Pa*), all the scales have both the *madhyamas* (perfect fourth and augmented fourth).

This system of thirty-six parent scales is also compatible with certain scales which do not fit within the current concept of seventy-two *melakartas*, such as the Locrian mode and the blues scale (both of which utilise the perfect and the augmented fourth, that is, M_1 and M_2), and North Indian *ragas* like Basant Bahaar (S M_1 P G_2 M_1 N_2 D_2 N_3 $\dot{S}$—$\dot{S}$ N_3 D_1 P M_2 G_3 R_1 S), Behag, Lalit, Gaud Sarang, Hameer and Shyam Kalyan, in which both the *madhyamas* are given equal prominence in the scale.

The seventy-two *melas* can be derived from the thirty-six by omitting M_2 in one set and the second thirty-two by omitting M_1. Further, using these scales in each semitone and octave we can get 36 x 36 = 1,296 scales.

Even though in our Indian system the same scale can be sung or played on an instrument in all the twelve semitones, if we give a name to that particular scale, it will be one name for all the twelve scales because the relative interval between the notes will be the same. However, when we play a particular scale on a piano, there will be slight differences between the notes played because the Indian method lays emphasis on relative pitch, which would vary with the tempered system of tuning. So, the 36 x 36 x 12 could theoretically be developed into *raga*s with minor variations of microtones. Incidentally, out of the seventy-two *mela*s, almost half could be derived by the *moorchana* method (modal shift of the tonic). So, as it is, shifting the tonic of the thirty-six scales can derive almost 50 per cent of the seventy-two *mela*s.

Harmony

Harmony is created by the successive combination of notes (known as 'chords'—three or more notes at a time) that are pleasing. This successive combination of notes moving one after another, known as chord progression, creates a vertical motion in an orchestral composition. This vertical motion supports the melodic structure, which is more linear. The melodic structure is a succession of single notes creating a melody. In some cases, there is more than one melodic line. The supportive melodic lines create what is known as counterpoint.

When creating compositions based on *Raga* Harmony, it might help to have some familiarity with whichever *raga* a composer is selecting for creating the harmony and the melody, so that the tonality and the intervals can create a strong flavour of the *raga*. This would allow any audience that is familiar with the *raga* concept to clearly hear and get the feeling of the *raga*, in addition to getting the Western harmonic sounds. It is essential for a composer to know the instrumentation of the orchestra, and also have knowledge of orchestration, harmony and harmonic progression in order to create a new platform and a new direction of music composition. Because of the innumerable possibilities of *ragas* in Carnatic music, it will be easier for different composers to create compositions that are totally unique, with totally different tonalities. It is possible to create different harmonic tonalities whenever one selects different *ragas*, and to create a composition using implied harmonies of the *ragas*. By this, some of the combinations of notes will fit into traditionally used chords, with specific names (like major, minor, diminished, augmented, suspended fourth, etc.). Some of the combinations of notes will create totally new chords, which have not been normally used or traditionally named.

In addition, by combining some of the notes, we can create clusters of tonality, which will sound different. Sometimes, to an untrained ear, harmonic compositions based on a *raga* might sound like they are based on the same tonality. This is partly due to a fundamental difference between Western classical and Indian classical music.

In Western classical music, compositions are written in a particular key such as E. A composition such as the *Bach Violin Partita* in E major is always played only in that key. Also, the Western violin is always tuned to GDAE, irrespective of the key of the composition.

In the Indian discipline, it is normal to have one particular note as the base tone (*Sa*) for the entire concert. Instruments are even tuned accordingly. For example, a violin could be tuned to D-A-D-A (if D is *Sa* and A is *Pa*) or E-B-E-B (if E is *Sa* and B is *Pa*). Some instruments like the flute, *mridangam*, *ghatam* or morsing are prepared and selected for different suitable pitches. So, normally, for an entire concert, the same tonic base (*Sa*) is maintained, supplementing it with a tambura, which is normally tuned to the tonic (*Sa*) and the dominant (*Pa*). The main artist normally chooses a convenient pitch. A composition created by Dikshithar (for example, *Vatapi Ganapathim*) can be performed in any pitch—it can be sung by a male singer in C or C# and a female singer in G or G# or violin, flute or *veena* in D or E, with any of these notes being the tonic or *Sa*.

In Western classical music, it is not uncommon to have different keys for different movements of compositions (for example, Tchaikovsky violin concerto in D major uses D major in Movement I and G minor in Movement II). These key changes make harmonic movement much more obvious and evident than when the tonal centre stays the same throughout the composition, although it is not necessarily 'more complex' or 'more harmonic'. Interestingly, in the Baroque style, it was common for composers like J.S. Bach to use tonality for an entire composition, using related major and minor keys (those with the same key signature). In Bach's violin concerto in A minor, he uses A minor for the first and third movements and the related C major for the second movement.

While composing Western classical compositions using *Raga* Harmony, therefore, it is advisable to use harmony that maintains the same tonal centre, so it retains the essence of the *raga* concept. Each movement can be in a different *raga*, but still maintain the same *Sa* or tonic. The lush harmonies, which can be created in this manner, can be not only unusual and pleasing but also complex and academically fascinating.

It is interesting to note that compositions created using *Raga* Harmony can be played by any normal Western classical orchestra around the world. No additional training of musicians is required, except perhaps for individual musicians making themselves comfortable with the physical expression of unusual scale patterns. There is no need for the individual musicians of an orchestra to understand the concept of *Raga* Harmony, as the composer will create the composition, and provide the notated scores of music for each individual musician to play.

It is also useful to point out at this juncture that while musicians and composers trained in Indian styles of music may be familiar with *raga* concepts and with hearing a melody line with microtonal ornamentation, they should train their ears to hear the multiple layers in a harmonic composition by listening for different lines.

With the possibilities of *Raga* Harmony, one can create new, fresh and unusual harmonies by using different notes of the scales, which have not been explored at all thus far. Harmonies are created normally by skipping notes and keeping, for example, tonic, third and fifth (major, minor, augmented or diminished triad, depending on the position of the third and fifth intervals). Additionally, we can create seventh chords, ninth chords, eleventh chords, thirteenth, etc., and also sixth chords, suspended fourth, and others. Composers like Arnold Schoenberg and Alexander Scriabin have used a series of intervals of fourths to create chords and some of them also used seconds. Debussy used clusters of tones to create different colours. All the varieties of compositions and harmonies which have been used will fit into this expanded system. The *Raga*

Harmony concept based on thirty-six scales will give enough original material to composers for centuries to come, since it is not possible for one person to master all the primary scales and all the possibilities of the millions of scales from that, the multimillion possibilities.

This research work can serve as a starting point, and further research can be done on the rhythmic possibilities, which are highly developed in Indian music, including the 175 *talas*, 108 *talas*, *Chapu talas*, Tiruppugazh *talas* and the Bhujangams of Adi Shankaracharya.

Further work can also be done using the *rasa* concept, which deals with various emotions and their portrayal by humans. The *rasa* concept, when applied alongside the *raga* concept, can be extended to *Raga* Harmony.

One can go much beyond talking about harmony using Western music—by considering it melodically, rhythmically and emotionally, creating different subtle emotions and flavours, and describing human beings through our *raga* system. When a Western composer studies this with his knowledge of harmony, we can reach a highly sophisticated degree of composition with the existing reservoir of emotional, rhythmic and melodic concepts, without compromising the Western concept of harmony, counterpoint and other tools.

References

- Bharatmuni. *The Nātya Śāstra of Bharatamuni.* Translated by a board of scholars. Orient Book Distributors, 2000.
- Bagchee, Sandeep. *Nād.* Mumbai: Eeshwar, 1998.
- Bailie, J.M. *The Da Capo History of Western Classical Music.* New York: Da Capo Press, 1999.
- Bandyopadhyaya, S. *The Origin of Rāga.* New Delhi: Munshiram Manoharlal, 1977.
- Bharata Muni and Manomohan Ghosh. *Natyasastra.* Calcutta: Manisha Granthalaya, 1956.
- Dattila and Mukunda Lāṭha. *Dattilam.* New Delhi: Indira Gandhi National Centre for the Arts, 1988.
- Deśapāṇḍe, Vāmana Harī. *Indian Musical Traditions.* Bombay: Popular Prakashan, 1973.
- Deva, Bigamudre Chaitanya. *Indian Music.* New Delhi: Indian Council for Cultural Relations, 1974.
- Dhandapani, M.N. and D. Paṭṭammāḷ. *Raga Pravaham.* Delhi: Central Natak Academy, 1984.
- Geetha, Ravikumar. *The Concept 7 Evolution of Raga in Hindustani and Karnatic Music.* Mumbai: Bharatiya Vidya Bhavan, 2002.
- Grout, Donald Jay and Claude V. Palisca. *A History of Western Music.* 9th edn. New York: Norton, 2014.

- Hindley, Geoffrey and Norbert Dufourcq. *Larousse Encyclopedia of Music*. London: Hamlyn, 1971.

- Iyengar, R. Rangaramanuja. *History of South Indian (Carnatic) Music, from Vedic Times to the Present*. Madras. 1972. [Copies can be had from Mrs. Padma Varadan, Bombay].

- Jairazbhoy, N.A. *The Ragas of North Indian Music Their Structure and Evolution*. London: Faber and Faber Ltd, 1971.

- Kaufmann, Walter. *The Ragas of North India*. Bloomington, Ind.: London, 1968.

- Kaufmann, Walter. *The Rāgas of South India*. Bloomington: Indiana University Press, 1977.

- Kitson, C.H. *Elementary Harmony*. Oxford: Clarendon Press, 1920.

- Logan, Jack. *Music in Our World*. 3rd edn. San Diego: McGraw Hill, 1992.

- Lovelock, William. *A Concise History of Music*. London: G. Bell & Sons, 1968.

- Matanga, Muni and Premalatā Śarmā. *Bṛhaddeśī of Śrī Mataṅga Muni*. New Delhi: Indira Gandhi National Centre for the Arts, 1992.

- Mudduveṅkaṭamakhin, and R. Sathyanarayana. *Rāgalakṣaṇam of Śrī Mudduveṅkaṭamakhin*. New Delhi: Indira Gandhi National Centre for the Arts in association with Motilal Banarsidass Publishers, Delhi, 2010.

- Paṇḍarīka Viṭṭhala, and R. Satyanarayana. *Nartananirṇaya of Paṇḍarīka Viṭṭhala*. New Delhi: Indira Gandhi National Centre for the Arts and Motilal Banarsidass Publishers, 1998.

- Pesch, Ludwig. *The Illustrated Companion to South Indian Classical Music*. Delhi: Oxford University Press, 1999.

- Prajnanananda, Swami. *Music of the Nations*. New Delhi: Munshiram Manoharlal Publishers, 1973.
- Ramanathan, N. *Musical Forms in Saṅgītaratnākara*. Chennai: Sampradāya, 1999.
- Rao, Pappu Venugopala. *Sangeeta Sampradaya Pradarsini of Brahmasri Subbarama Diksitulu*. Chennai: The Music Academy, 2013.
- Sambamoorthy, P. *South Indian Music*—Vol. 1. Madras: Indian Music Pub. House, 1966.
- Sambamoorthy, P. *South Indian Music*—Vol. 2. Madras: Indian Music Pub. House, 1954.
- Sambamoorthy, P. *South Indian Music*—Vol. 3. Madras: Indian Music Pub. House, 1958.
- Sambamoorthy, P. *South Indian Music*—Vol. 4. Madras: Indian Music Pub. House, 1960.
- Sambamoorthy, P. *South Indian Music*—Vol. 5. Madras: Indian Music Pub. House, 1963.
- Sambamurthy, P. *Elements of Western Music for Students of Indian Music*. Madras: The Indian Music Publishing House, 1982.
- Subramaniam, L. and Viji Subramaniam. *Euphony*. New Delhi: Affiliated East-West Press, 1995.
- Sundaram, B.M. *Palaiyazhi*. Madras, Tamil Nadu: Murali Ravali Art Centre, 1979.
- Sundaram Iyer, A. *Shree Muthuswami Dikshitar Keerthanaigal*. Madras: Music Book Publishers.
- Sundaravadivelu, N.D. 'Orchestra with Special Reference to South Indian Music'. *Bulletin of the Institute of Traditional Cultures, Music*. July–December 1973.
- Varadarajan, Brinda. 'Music in the Sama Veda'. *The Journal of the Madras Music Academy*, LVIII (1987): 169–180.

- Veṅkaṭamakhi, and R. Sathyanarayana. *Caturdaṇḍīprakāśikā*. New Delhi: Indira Gandhi National Centre for the Arts in association with Motilal Banarsidass Publishers, Delhi, 2002.
- Wade, Bonnie C. *Music in India*. Englewood Cliffs, N.J.: Prentice-Hall, 1979.

Appendix

Major Orchestral Works of
Dr L. Subramaniam

Concertos

Double Concerto for Violin & Flute (1984)

Fantasy on Vedic Chants (1985)

Nada Priya (1986)

Turbulence Concerto (1987)

Shanti Priya (1988)

Paris Concerto (2015)

Isabella Violin Concerto (2016)

Symphonies

Global Symphony (1995)

Astral Symphony (1996)

Turbulence Symphony (2006)

Freedom Symphony (2007)

Sai Symphony (2015)

Datta Symphony (2017)

Symphony of Celebrations (2017)

Bharat Symphony (2017)
Mahatma Symphony (2022)
Navagraha Symphony

Other Works

Spring Rhapsody (1986)
Beyond (1991)
Flight of the Humble Bee (2016)
Tribute to Bach (2016)
Violins for Peace (2016)
Meera Bhajans (2018)
Reflections
Transformation
Conversations